Creative Crafts for Creative Hands

PATCHWORK &
QUILTING

CHARTWELL BOOKS
a division of Book Sales, Inc.
POST OFFICE BOX 7100
114 Northfield Avenue
Edison, NJ 08818-7100

CLB 4124
© 1995 CLB Publishing, Godalming, Surrey
Printed and bound in Proost N.V., Belgium
All rights reserved
ISBN 0-7858-0127-8

Managing Editor: Jo Finnis
Editors: Sue Wilkinson; Geraldine Christy
Jacket and prelim design: Art of Design
Typesetting: Litho Link Ltd, Welshpool, Powys
Production: Ruth Arthur; Sally Connolly; Neil Randles; Karen Staff; Jonathan Tickner; Matthew Dale
Director of Production: Gerald Hughes

Photographers
Jacket Marie-Louise Avery/Eaglemoss; Jacket flap Steve Tanner/Eaglemoss; Title page Graham Rae/Eaglemoss; 9 Ariadne Holland; 10 (l) American Museum in Britain; 10 (r) Ariadne Holland; 11 (t) Elizabeth Whiting Associates; 11 (b) Richard Paul; 12 (l) American Museum in Britain; 12 (r) Marie Claire Idees; 13 (t) Robert Harding Syndication/IPC Magazines; 13 (b) Ariadne Holland; 14 (t) Jane Churchill; 14 (b) American Museum in Britain; 15-16 Ariadne Holland; 17-18 Ariadne Holland; 19-21 Ariadne Holland 23-24 Steve Tanner/Eaglemoss; 25 Ariadne Holland; 27-28 Graham Rae/Eaglemoss; 29 Ariadne Holland; 32 Ariadne Holland; 33-38 Marie-Louise Avery/Eaglemoss; 39-40 Marie-Louise Avery/Eaglemoss; 42 Marie-Louise Avery/Eaglemoss; 43 Ariadne Holland; 44 House and Interiors; 46 Bill McLaughlin; 47 Ariadne Holland; 51-52 Jahres Zeiten Verlag; 53 Pictures Colour Library; 56 Elizabeth Whiting Associates; 57 Anna French; 58-59 Osborne and Little; 60 Steve Tanner/Eaglemoss

Illustrators
15-16 John Hutchinson; 18 Clare Clements, Terry Evans; 20-22 Terry Evans; 23-24 John Hutchinson; 26 Terry Evans; 28 Kate Simunek; 30-32 John Hutchinson; 34-38 John Hutchinson; 40-42 John Hutchinson; 44-46 John Hutchinson; 48-50 John Hutchinson; 52 John Hutchinson 54-56 Terry Evans; 58-60 John Hutchinson

Creative Crafts for Creative Hands

PATCHWORK &
QUILTING

*How to make beautiful gifts and objects for the home,
from basic techniques to finishing touches.*

CHARTWELL
BOOKS, INC.

Contents

Piecing together patchwork

Patchwork has long been identified with a simple, country way of life, combining fine craftsmanship with thrifty recycling. Now this traditional craft has become an important decorative form with many uses in the home.

The term patchwork is used to describe the joining of shaped pieces of patterned or coloured fabrics to form a cloth mosaic. It is a technique that offers limitless scope for experimenting with pattern, colour and texture.

▼ A throw of many colours
This exquisite, gaily coloured patchwork quilt is a modern rendition of the famous baskets pattern, which makes good use of triangular pieces of all sizes.

9

Types of patchwork

Patchwork can be divided into two broad categories. In pieced work, small, regularly shaped scraps of material are sewn together to form a strong fabric. Because the patches are stitched to each other rather than to a background fabric, pieced work must be lined to hide all the raw edges at the back.

In applied patchwork or appliqué, motifs are cut from plain or decorative fabrics. The edges are turned under and the pieces are hemmed or slipstitched to a background fabric. Sometimes the edges are left raw and buttonhole stitch is used to join the fabric to the base in a more elaborate way.

The pattern-making possibilities offered by patchwork are almost infinite, but the traditional patterns are still the most popular. The simplest patchworks are one-patch designs based on a single geometric shape such as a triangle, a square or a hexagon. Beautiful effects can be achieved by using different fabrics to create patterns. For instance, in the tumbling blocks design, light, dark and middle tones are used to create a three-dimensional illusion.

In the last half of the nineteenth century, crazy patchwork became fashionable. Scraps of unrelated fabrics, silks, ribbons, satins or velvet, were sewn on to a backing. Each piece was outlined with feather stitching in thick silk, often in a golden thread. Crazy patchwork was used for quilts, table coverings, cushions, handkerchiefs and nightdress cases.

▲ Pioneer spirit
The log cabin pattern is one of the most basic and popular forms of patchwork, taking its name from the straight strips used to make it. The final effect depends upon the arrangement of colours.

▶ A joy to behold
The ingenuity of patchwork patterns can be astounding. Looking closely at this quilted throw, sometimes your eye will rest on the circles; at others, you can make out patched squares.

United States of patchwork

Some of the loveliest patchwork comes from the United States, where it is a popular folk craft. The earliest American quilts were made for protection against the harsh New World winters and based on the patterns used in Europe. As time passed, the colonists developed their own style. Indeed, the names given to many of the patterns – log cabin, barn raising, bear's paw and cactus basket – reflect their origins.

In particular, they evolved the block method of working, in which a series of rectangular or square units were made up separately and then stitched together to create a large quilt. The advantage was that the individual blocks were more manageable to work than one large quilt. Sometimes quilts were worked by several different people and became known as friendship quilts. Each individual would work a separate block, often in a different design. The skill came in assembling these independent blocks into an amazing pattern.

On many old quilts you will find a spider's web embroidered in a corner, as recognition of the creature's skill. In some areas a spider's web would be laid on the back of a baby girl's hand so that she would acquire some of that dexterity. Often, too, you will find a deliberate error in a patchwork, such as a repeating motif worked in the wrong colour. This reflected a belief that only God could create perfection and it was therefore inappropriate for a mere mortal to aspire to such heights.

▲ Suffolk puffs
Here, small circles of gathered fabric, called Suffolk puffs, have been stitched together to form a multi-coloured mosaic of a table-cover. Note how a diamond-pattern has been superimposed within an otherwise haphazard arrangement of the patchwork puffs by carefully planning the criss-cross of pink pieces.

◀ Matrimonial bliss
A double wedding ring quilt was traditionally made by a mother as a wedding gift for her son or daughter. Blue and pink fabrics were usually associated with this pattern as a symbol of the union between a man and a woman. Sometimes the patchwork pieces were cut from remnants of fabric from childhood dresses.

11

▲ Award winner
A pretty medallion quilt is one of the simplest to make, by surrounding a central piece with five borders.

◄ Bar-coded
The Amish produce colourful, abstract bar designs that have a very modern feel and are enormously popular.

Making patchwork

The whole idea of the patchwork effect is bound to appeal to anyone who enjoys making patterns with shapes and colours. However, while some may regard sewing their own patchwork as a relaxing recreation or a labour of love, to others the prospect is merely daunting.

Fortunately, for the latter group a great many patchwork designs can be done on a modern sewing machine. Before the advent of the sewing machine in the 1850s, all patchwork was done by hand. In country areas, the entire family contributed, several generations of women working to stitch the pieces together, with children perfecting their plain sewing stitches on patchwork squares or hexagons, while the men cut templates for the patches. The work they produced was often simple but practical, invaluable for use as warm bedcovers.

Working out the patterns

Patchwork patterns work on many levels, from umpteen tiny pieces collected into incredibly intricate patterns to far less complicated designs on a much broader scale. Some appliquéd quilts are worked with complicated pictorial motifs and many include symbols. The Pennsylvania Dutch of North America favoured bright colours and pictorial motifs and symbols, often including the pineapple, a popular token of welcome and hospitality.

Seminole patchwork – devised originally by the Seminole Indians of North America at the turn of the century – is one of the easiest and quickest to make on a machine. Basically it consists of strips of different patterned and plain materials joined to make a whole sheet of fabric. This is then cut into strips again at an angle to the original strips. These new strips can be rearranged into fresh patterns and machine-stitched together.

All sorts of fabric are suitable for making patchwork, with the proviso that it is better not to mix fabrics of different weights and raw materials. One appealing idea is to collect a selection of fabrics from the country you are visiting on a holiday abroad and use them to make a patchwork of your travels when you get home again. For another memento-style patchwork, you could save remnants of materials used for the dresses on your wedding day to make cushions or a throw for your bedroom.

You can skip the patchwork-making phase of a patchwork quilt altogether by buying pretty fabrics with a convincing, ready printed patchwork design. These can look lovely and provide a simple way of introducing an individual look into a contemporary home.

Using patchwork

Patchwork can play many roles in the country home. The most beautiful and valuable can be used as wall hangings, where they will add a wonderful splash of colour to the room. Probably the most familiar uses are as bedcovers and throws, but the effect also works well on smaller items like cushions, table-cloths, curtains and chair covers.

Cushions are a terrific way of practising your patchwork skills on an achievable scale. Use a crazy patchwork technique enriched with embroidery for a novel effect. Covering the top of a blanket box with foam or wadding and a patchwork cover is easy to do.

When recombining two pairs of curtains to make a new pair, look for interesting fabric combinations, like mixing old velvet found at a jumble sale with some rich tapestry or damask. Cut the curtains into squares or rectangles; for a particularly stylish effect you can trim the patches so that they decrease in height up the curtain. For a variation on the theme, join horizontal or vertical strips of varying widths.

You could even patchwork sheers to create unusual, floaty curtains. Cut squares of lace and spotted voile or muslin. Stitch the squares together on the right side, covering the seams with thin ribbon, maybe in a pale pastel shade.

A Roman blind can be another very good way of showing off a piece of fine patchwork. The seams and stitching will have to be strong and neat as they will need to take a certain amount of weight and may be visible. Bordering it in a frame of the main colour looks dramatic.

▲ All square
A patchwork pattern created from large pieces can look remarkably effective on a quilted bedspread like this.

◄ From rags to riches
These two charming patchwork cushions show what can be achieved with a few scraps of fabric and a little imagination. The triangular pattern is an example of pieced work, where the patches have been sewn together to form the cover. The heart shapes, on the other hand, demonstrate applied patchwork, having been sewn to the plain cover and then lightly quilted around the heart shape.

◄ Patchy prints
One artful way of bringing patchwork into the home is to use fabrics that are already printed with a patched pattern. Here, a full-colour Dutch tulip print has been alternated with its negative in pink and white for a patchwork effect. Note how the second fabric, inspired by old Delft tiles, also contrives to look like a patchwork.

▼ United nations
Making a patchwork becomes a social activity when a group of needleworkers share the sewing of a friendship quilt. This one depicts the floral emblems of the original thirteen states of the American Union with the national emblems of England, Wales, Scotland and Ireland arranged as a border.

Patchwork quilts

One of the most popular uses of both types of patchwork is as a top for a quilt. Indeed, the terms quilting and patchwork are frequently used interchangeably. In addition to making snug bedspreads, patchwork quilts can be handy as throws to drape casually over a screen or the back of a settee or chair. Used as a table-cloth, a thin quilt can also provide good protection for a valuable or vulnerable table-top.

A quilt is really a textile sandwich, with a top layer of fabric, which may be plain or printed but looks so much more interesting and traditional if it is made from a sheet of pieced or applied patchwork. The bottom layer is generally plain and there is usually a wadding filling to provide warmth and some substance for the quilting technique.

The quilting consists of creating a pattern in running stitch, which also holds the layers together. The quilted design may relate to the patchwork pattern, following the outline of appliquéd pieces for example, or it may be an unrelated, repeating pattern worked over the entire surface, like the familiar stitched diamond lattice.

In the old days, patchwork top covers were almost always quilted for warmth. These days patchwork covers are often used as decorative bedcovers rather than for warmth, so they are simply lined. However, if you do make a patchwork bedcover, you should really consider quilting it.

TRIANGULAR TREE

Materials

Selection of plain and patterned cotton fabrics for the patchwork

21cm (8in) square of firmly woven cotton or calico to use as the backing

Fine dowel or **slim, straight twig**

Double-sided red ribbon

Washable filling

Small basket filled with florist's foam and **moss**

Ruler and **sharp scissors**

Matching sewing threads

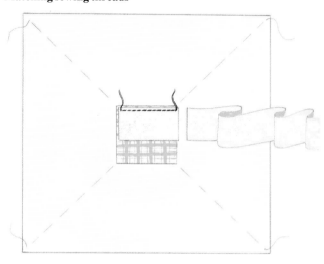

These unusual patchwork trees are made by stitching fine fabric strips on to backing fabric – a technique known as log cabin patchwork. You can hang them on your tree, or stiffen them with a dowel and 'plant' them in a small basket. Work to one set of measurements only.

1 Getting started Fold your backing square in half diagonally in both directions. Tack along the folds. Cut a 5cm (2in) square of patterned fabric, and centre it over the backing square. Tack in place, 5mm (¼in) in from the small square's edge. Mark up 3cm (1¼in) wide strips across your patterned fabrics, marking along the straight grain. Cut out the strips – these will be trimmed to length as you stitch them in place.

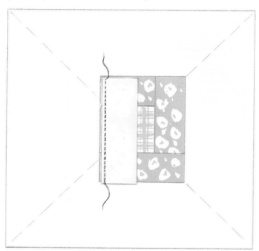

2 Attaching the strips With right sides facing, lay one of the patterned strips along the top edge of the central square, matching the top edge and one side edge. Taking a 5mm (¼in) seam allowance, stitch the strip in place along the top edge. Stop stitching at the edge of the central square, and trim the strip to line up with the square's edge. Fold back the strip to lie right side up, against the backing fabric.

▼ *Cleverly displayed These delightful patchwork Christmas trees can be stood upright in a pot or basket, or hung on your tree.*

3 Finishing the square Take the same patterned strip and lay it down the right-hand side of the central square and border, with right sides facing. Stitch in place as before, taking a 5mm (¼in) seam allowance. Trim the strip, then use it to border the lower edge and the left-hand edge of the square in the same way. Use a differently patterned strip to add another set of borders around the central square exactly as before, taking a 5mm (¼in) seam allowance each time. The tacked diagonals will help you position the strips accurately. Repeat to add two more sets of borders, so you reach the edge of the backing square. Press.

4 Making up the tree With right sides facing, fold the patchwork square in half diagonally and stitch up the sides, leaving a small opening. Turn right side out and insert filling, then slipstitch closed. For hanging decorations, insert a ribbon into the triangle's top point as you stitch the seam. For stand-up trees, snip a small hole halfway across the bottom edge and insert the dowel. Tie a ribbon around the dowel and stick it into the basket of florist's foam. Cover the top with moss.

PATCHWORK BALLS

Materials

Selection of plain and patterned cotton fabrics
Double-sided red ribbon
Washable filling
Mediumweight wadding
Dressmaker's carbon paper or iron-on transfer pencil
Stiff card to make templates
Long, slim dowel, with one end sharpened to a point
Small basket and matching sewing threads

Like the patchwork tree triangles on page 15, the patchwork balls used to create this Christmas tree can also be used as hanging decorations.

1 Cutting out Trace off the large, medium and small pattern pieces given opposite on to card. Cut out. Draw around each template six times on to your fabrics, and cut out. Use the medium-sized template to mark up another twelve shapes on the fabrics, and six on wadding, for the leaves. Cut out. Each template is designed to include a seam allowance.

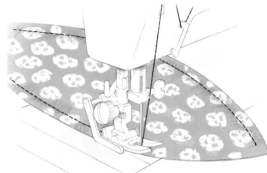

2 Making up the balls Take two of the smallest pattern pieces, and put them together with right sides facing and edges matching. Stitch the two together down one side, taking a 5mm (¼in) seam allowance. Join on the remaining four segments of the same size in the same way. Then put the first and last segments together, with right sides facing, and stitch two thirds of the way up the side edge. Snip into all the seam allowances so they will lie flat, then turn through to the right side.

3 Completing the balls Insert the filling through the opening, then slipstitch it closed. Leave small openings at the top and bottom of the sphere for the dowel to pass through. Repeat to make up the two other patchwork balls.

4 Making leaves Match fabric leaves into pairs, right sides facing, and lay over wadding leaves. Stitch together, leaving an opening. Turn right side out and stitch closed. Quilt around leaves, close to edge.

5 Assembling the tree Make up a small dove in one of your patterned fabrics, as for the *Festive basket*. Insert the dowel through all three balls in order of size, starting with the largest, and then slide it into the dove. Tie a ribbon around the dowel, just below the dove.

Hold the dove and balls firmly in place by sewing them together with a few tiny stitches around the dowel. Arrange the leaves in the basket, so they fan out decoratively, and sit the 'tree' on top. If you find that the leaves fall out, hold them in place on the dowel with a few stitches.

◀ *Patchwork pile-up*
In this imaginative design, patchwork balls in different sizes are piled up on top of one another, to form a Christmas tree. The tree is 'planted' in a small wicker basket, and crowned with a red ribbon and a dove.

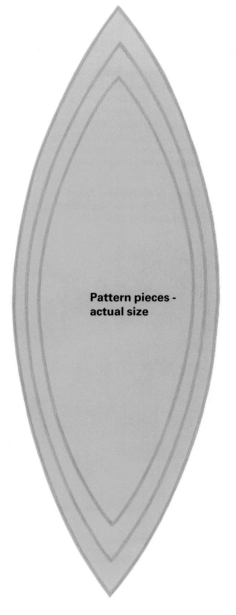

Pattern pieces - actual size

Squares bedcover

Patchwork bedcovers can be made with new cottons, but they have much more charm if made from old blouses, dresses and curtains. The fabrics will have a soft and mellow quality, laced with memories (traditionally quilts were made with recycled cloth).

This patchwork cover is machine stitched with squares of pastel colours. Every now and then a cross-stitched rose, worked on a background of easy-to-count aida fabric, is inserted for interest. (Aida is an evenweave cotton for cross-stitch embroidery.) You could achieve the same effect by choosing a fabric with an isolated floral motif on a pale background.

The cover shown is made up of 225 patches, measures 200 cm (80 in) square and is designed for a single bed. However, you can make the cover to any size depending on the number of squares you make. For example, a child's cot quilt, measuring 100 x 120cm (39 x 47in), would take 56 patches.

Materials
Pastel fabrics, oddments in plains and patterns for the patches
Plain cotton sheeting fabric, 2.5m (2³/₄yd) of 228cm (90in) wide, for backing and borders
Card for template
Matching sewing thread
Optional: White aida with 14 blocks 2.5cm (1in) – 50cm (5/8yd) of 130cm (50in) wide
> **DMC stranded cotton** in dark pink 601, pink 603, light pink 605, green 958
> **Dressmaker's chalk**

◀ **The completed patchwork**
Scattered among the fabric patches are squares of evenweave cotton, each embroidered with a single rose.

TO MAKE THE PATCHWORK

1 Embroidered squares If you choose to include these, cut the aida into 24 pieces each 16cm (6¼in) square. Following the chart and key, work the rose motif centrally on each square. Use four strands of stranded cotton and work in cross stitch over two blocks of aida. When the embroidery is complete, with the motif centrally placed, trim each square down to 14cm (5½in).

2 Cutting the squares Draw up a 14cm (5½in) square template from card and cut out. Using the card template, mark and cut out 201 squares of fabric (or 225 if you are not using the embroidered squares). Mark on the wrong side of the different fabrics, keeping the template edges straight on the fabric grain.

3 Arranging the colours Spread out all the squares (including the embroidered ones) on a flat surface, 15 squares by 15 squares. Move them about until you are pleased with the design. Mark on the wrong side of each square its position in the arrangement.

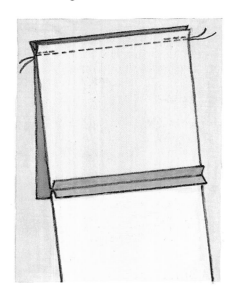

4 Stitching the patches Pin and machine stitch the first row of 15 squares together, making absolutely sure that the seam allowance is consistently 1cm (⅜in). Place the patches back to back with right sides together; pin and stitch, working a few stitches in reverse at each end to fasten stitches. Press seams open. Make up the remaining rows of 15 squares in the same way, pressing the seams open.

KEY

Each square of the diagram is equal to 2 blocks of aida.

Suggested colours only; choose colours to match your own patches.

- ⊙ **Green 958**
- ⊠
- ⊙ **Dark pink 601**
- ⊡ **Pink 603**

Light pink 605

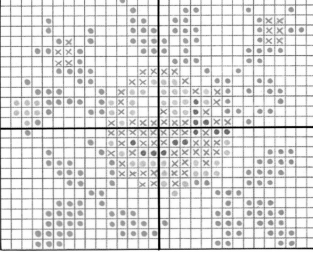

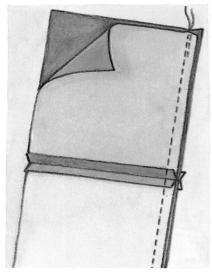

5 Making a block Pin and stitch the rows together to form a block 182cm (72 ¾in) square, taking 1cm (⅜in) seam allowance. Press seams open.

6 Making the border From sheeting, cut four strips, each 202cm x 12cm (80 x 4 ¾in). With right sides together, pin and stitch a strip to one side of the patchwork. Starting a short distance from the corner, stitch, leaving a 1cm (⅜in) seam, to within a short distance of next corner. Repeat for all sides.

Adding backing
For warmth, add a layer of curtain interlining, bump or domette, with the backing. Join widths with a conventional flat seam or overlap edges and oversew. Catchstitch through the layers to hold in place.

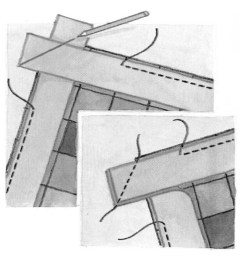

7 Mitring the corners At each corner, to form a mitre, mark diagonally across the border strips, from corner to corner, as shown. Fold the border strips with right sides together, pin and stitch along the marked line. Trim and press open. Complete stitching the border to the patchwork at the corners.

8 The backing Cut a piece of sheeting 202cm (81in) square. Lay it on top of the patchwork, right sides facing. Pin and stitch together all round, with 1cm (⅜in) seam allowance and leave a 20cm (8in) opening along one edge. Trim and turn right side out. Turn in opening edges in line with remainder of the seam; slipstitch to close.

Pennsylvania patchwork

Cunning combinations of traditional sewing skills often give stunning results. Here, we've teamed the art of patchwork with cross stitch embroidery to create two of these wonderful fresh-looking cushion covers.

The distinctive designs are derived from traditional American patchwork motifs. The heart cushion is made up from a series of plain and mini-checked fabric squares. The five plain squares

have been embroidered with cross stitch hearts to create an attractive Shaker-style effect. The house featured on the other cushion cover has been taken from a popular patchwork design called schoolhouses, but this house is worked in cross stitch rather than patchwork.

Match your patchwork fabrics and threads before you work the embroidery to ensure that the finished cushions will be as stylish as these.

▲ Favourite fabrics
Since mini-checked fabrics are so fashionable at the moment, it should be relatively easy to find inexpensive remnants, ideal for these patchwork cushions. However, if you do have problems finding checked fabrics in suitable shades of dusty pink and blue, you could always substitute tiny sprig prints instead, or even use a small all-over floral print in similar colours.

CUSHION WITH HEART MOTIFS

Materials

White evenweave linen 66 x 46cm (26 x 18in) with 27 threads to 2.5cm (1in)

Checked fabric, four 14cm (5½in) squares in four different designs and colourways

DMC pearl cotton No 5 in the following colours: 1 skein each of ecru, dusty pink 223, pale dusty pink 224, blue 322, salmon pink 352, green 368, pale salmon pink 754 and light blue 3325

Embroidery needle size 6

Backing fabric 38cm (15¼in) square

Cushion pad 36cm (14in) square

Matching sewing thread

Embroidery frame (optional)

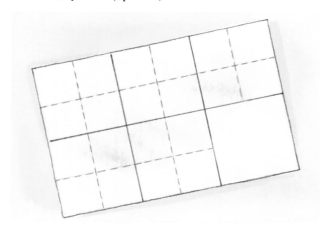

1 Preparing the linen Embroider all the hearts on to the same piece of linen, before cutting the linen up into individual squares. Divide the linen in half lengthways, then mark out five 20cm (8in) squares, one for each heart. To provide a guide for the stitching, tack across the centre of each heart area, lengthways and widthways, using a dark coloured thread. Set the linen into the embroidery frame.

▲ Have a heart
These stitched hearts look superb set against white fabric, and checked patches add a flourish.

2 Embroidering hearts Each heart is stitched in cross stitch using pearl cotton and working over three threads of linen. Each square on the diagram on page 22 denotes one cross stitch worked over three threads of linen. Follow the diagram and key for colours and position of stitches.

3 Finishing the hearts When all the hearts have been embroidered, cut out each one following the tacked lines. With the heart centrally placed, trim each square to 14cm (5½in). Either oversew round the raw edges or zigzag stitch on the sewing machine to prevent fraying. Press gently on the wrong side without flattening the stitches.

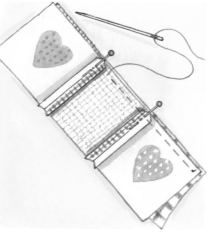

4 Planning the cushion front Lay out the embroidered and fabric squares in the arrangement shown. Then pin and stitch the squares together into lengthways strips, taking 1cm (⅜in) seam allowance. Stitch two embroidered hearts on either side of a central fabric square. Repeat to make up the two remaining strips. Press seams open.

5 Making up cushion front Pin and then stitch the three strips together to form the cushion front. Check the picture to ensure you have the strips in the correct order. It is also a good idea to place a pin horizontally in each seam across the joining seamlines so when the seam is stitched the squares will match each other exactly.

6 Completing the cushion Place the cushion front to the backing fabric with right sides together. Pin and stitch the edges together all the way round, leaving an opening centrally in the base edge. Trim seams and turn the cushion cover right side out. Then insert the cushion pad. Turn in the opening edges and slipstitch together to close.

HOUSE CUSHION

Materials

White evenweave linen with 27 threads to 2.5cm (1in): one piece 24cm (9½in) square and one piece 40 x 24cm (16 x 9½in)

Check fabric, 30 x 15cm (12 x 6in) in red, multi-check and blue

DMC pearl cotton No 5 in the following colours: ecru, blue 322, salmon pink 352, green 368 and light blue 3325

Embroidery needle size 6

Backing fabric 38cm (15¼in) square

Cushion pad 36cm (14in) square

Matching sewing thread

1 Preparing the linen Use the 24cm (9½in) square of linen for the house motif. Tack across the centre of the square both ways to provide guide lines for the stitching.

2 Embroidering a house Set the linen in the embroidery frame and work the house motif in cross stitch using pearl cotton. Each square on the diagram on page 22 represents one cross stitch worked over three threads of linen. Follow the diagram and key for colours and position of stitches. Complete by working the small corner motifs. Remove linen from frame and trim to 14cm (5½in) square. Oversew raw edges to prevent fraying. Press.

◄ **Going home**
This wonderful house has its own little heart which has been included in the design. Once the cross stitch embroidery is completed the cushion is quick and easy to make.

3 Preparing for the border strips Use the remaining piece of linen for the border strips. Tack across the centre, then divide each piece in half again to mark the four border areas. Then tack centrally across all four strips, to provide a guide for the stitching.

4 Embroidering border strips Set the border linen into the frame and work each section in cross stitch using pearl cotton. Each square on the diagram on page 22 represents one cross stitch worked over three threads of linen. Follow the diagram for colours and placement of stitches. When each strip is complete, cut out each piece. With the motif centrally placed trim to 14 x 7cm (5½ x 2¾in). Oversew edges.

5 Adding fabric strips From multi-check fabric cut out two strips each 14 x 7 cm (5½ x 2¾in) and four 7cm (2¾in) squares. Then pin and stitch one strip to the top and one to the base edges of house square, taking 1cm (⅜in) seam allowance. Press the seams open. Pin and stitch an embroidered strip to the opposite edge of check strip.

6 Completing border For the other check border, cut eight 7cm (2¾in) squares from blue check, and four 7cm (2¾in) squares and two strips 14 x 7cm (5½ x 2¾in) from red check fabric. Make up two lengthways strips: red square, blue square, red strip, blue square, red square. Press, then pin and stitch strips on either side of house.

7 Finishing the cushion The two remaining outside strips are made up from four remaining squares and remaining embroidered border strips. Pin and stitch together in the order shown. Press seams open. Then stitch each strip to the outside edge of the cushion. Press seams open. Complete cushion cover as in heart cushion step 6.

HEARTS CHART

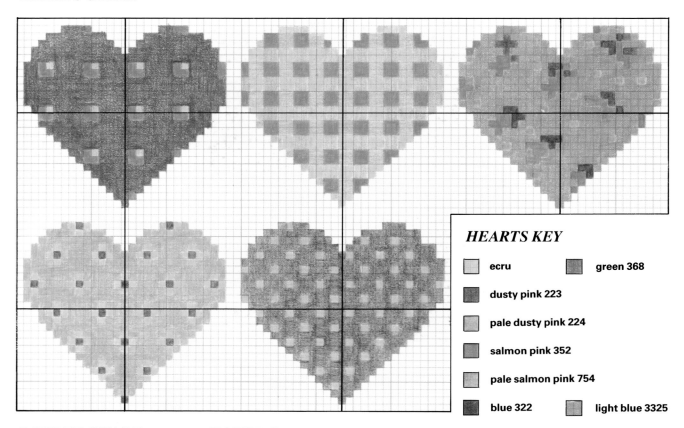

HEARTS KEY

☐	ecru	☐	green 368
☐	dusty pink 223		
☐	pale dusty pink 224		
☐	salmon pink 352		
☐	pale salmon pink 754		
☐	blue 322	☐	light blue 3325

BORDER CHART   HOUSE CHART

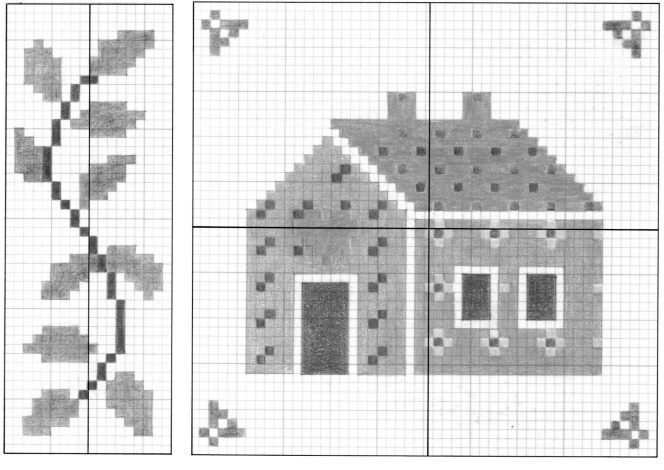

HOUSE/BORDER KEY

☐	ecru	☐	blue 322	☐	light blue 3325	☐	green 368	☐	salmon pink 352

Patchwork baskets

Mix and match small scraps of cotton fabric together to make these tiny patchwork baskets. Perfect for any occasion, you could use yellow and white fabrics and fill with miniature eggs for Easter or deep red fabrics filled with chocolate coins for Christmas.

As unique party bags for children, they could hold tiny presents and be played with afterwards. Take care not to use a large print fabric as it is less effective than a small design and the motifs will lose their impact. When using a motif fabric, make sure that the shapes lie diagonally and fit into a 3cm (1¼in) square. Use a fine print or plain fabric for the lining to complement any patterns used within the patchwork.

▲ Baskets of fun
These little handmade baskets make unique and useful table decorations and your guests will be delighted with the novel idea. Once made, these baskets can be used over and over again or as a gift wrapping for an extra special present.

Materials

Medium-weight cotton polyester fabric an assortment of fabric scraps for the eight small patches; 7cm (2¾in) square for base, 3 x 13cm (1¼ x 5¼in) for handle 13cm (5¼in) square for lining

Firm iron-on interfacing 35 x 42cm (14 x 16½in)

Sewing thread to match main colour of fabric scraps and contrasting colour for tacking

Ruler

Set square

Dressmaker's pencil

Fabric scissors

▶ **Layout diagram**
If you follow the arrows to sew up the patchwork you should end up with a little basket.

MAKING THE PATCHWORK BASKET

1 Preparing the fabric Make sure the fabric is clean. Iron and lay out flat to avoid creasing.

2 Cutting the patches Frame any motifs diagonally and using the dressmaker's pencil and set square, mark out eight patches on to the fabric scraps, each 4cm (1½in) square, then cut them out. To check the fabrics work well together, lay out the patches and base following the layout diagram.

3 Cutting the interfacing Using the dressmaker's pencil, ruler and set square, mark out eight patches 3cm (1¼in) square, one 6cm (2¼in) square and a strip 1 x 13cm (⅜ x 5¼in) on the right side of the interfacing.

4 Stiffening patches With wrong sides together, centre the interfacing squares on the fabric pieces. Then using a damp pressing cloth and warm iron, bond the interfacing on to the fabric to stiffen it.

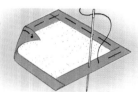

5 Neaten the patches Fold the raw edges to wrong side over the edge of the interfacing. Tack raw edges in place then using a damp pressing cloth and warm iron, press to sharpen the edges.

6 Stiffening the strip With wrong sides together, place the interfacing strip in the centre of the fabric strip and match the short ends to those of the fabric strip, then press as for the patches.

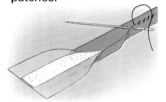

7 Neatening the strip Fold one long raw edge of strip to wrong side along the interfacing and press. Turn the remaining long raw edge to the wrong side to form a narrow double hem and press. With small stitches, slip-stitch the hem into place.

8 Placing the patches Lay the basket base with the right side facing up. Following the directions of the motifs, place the patches around the base as shown in the layout diagram.

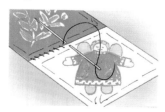

9 Joining the patches Taking a few threads of fabric from each folded edge, use small neat stitches to oversew the patches together.

10 Making the basket Following the diagram arrows, join the side of the smaller patches to form the basket sides and base.

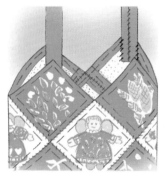

11 Attaching the handle With the hemmed edge of the handle to the inside, stitch 1cm (⅜in) of the handle ends to the two opposite patch points.

12 Lining the basket Fold a 6mm (¼in) hem to wrong side of the lining fabric square and tack to neaten. Hem in place and press. With wrong sides together, match the corners of the lining to the points of the patches along the upper edge of the basket. Pleating the lining at each corner, use small slip stitches to sew in place. Remove all tacking stitches.

tip

Alternative handles Handles can be made using a wide variety of materials such as ribbon threaded through Broderie Anglaise, ribbon or braid. When using an alternative material such as above, use two layers with wrong sides together, stiffening one with iron-on interfacing.

Patchwork picture

Pictures made with patchwork have a crafted individual look because any collection of patches is rarely cut from exactly the same fabrics. Even the choice of colour makes a vast difference to the look of the patchwork. Darker fabrics give a rich, warm and sumptuous look while softer muted colours give a prettier summery feel.

You can have enormous fun choosing and collecting fabrics to mix and match for this picture, but it's worth remembering that fabrics with small prints always look best. A patchwork picture is a timeless piece of art that you will never tire of and if you use fabrics from old clothes, it can hold many happy memories. The picture is lightly padded using wadding then quilted to achieve a slight three-dimensional effect. The finished size of the patchwork is 32 x 42cm (12½ x 16½in).

▼ Picture that
A patchwork flower posy makes a super picture, but you could make a patchwork of your home instead.

MAKING THE PICTURE

Materials

White cotton or linen fabric 32 x 42cm (12½ x 16½in)
Cream cotton or linen fabric 32 x 42cm (12½ x 16½in)
Printed cotton fabric scraps in blues, pinks, greens and creams
Lightweight iron-on interfacing
Lightweight wadding 32 x 42cm (12½ x 16½in)
Sewing thread cream and white
Calico 50 x 60cm (20 x 23½in)
Thin card for templates
Pencil
Sharp craft scissors
Dressmaker's carbon paper
Embroidery needle size 7
Stranded embroidery cotton to match cream fabric

1 Enlarge the motif Increase the size of the diagram **A** so one square measures 3cm (1¼in). Iron fabrics to remove creases and press interfacing to the back of patterned fabric scraps. Using the dressmaker's carbon paper transfer the enlarged motif on to the centre of the cream fabric.

2 Make the card templates Trace the triangle pattern **B**, and the individual petals, leaves, stems and basket handle from **A** on to the card. Mark an `X' on the right side of each shape, then adding 6mm (¼in) all round each shape for seams, cut out.

3 Cut out the fabric pieces With the right side uppermost, draw round each template on the right side of the selected patterned fabrics. Cut out eighteen of the triangular patches and one each of the others.

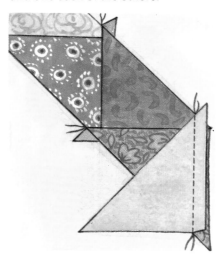

4 Making the basket Matching the shorter sides, stitch a row of seven triangular patches together, a row of five and two rows of three. Press seams open, then stitch rows together to form the basket.

5 Appliqué the picture Turn and tack the seam allowance to wrong side around each fabric shape and press. Snip seam allowance around curves, then beginning with the basket and following the traced pattern, use tiny slipstitches to stitch shapes in place on the cream fabric.

6 Finish the motif Finish the centre motif by embroidering your initial and adding a fabric bow.

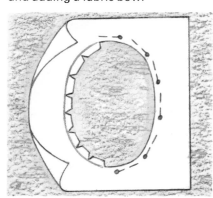

7 Cut the white fabric Transfer the oval shape around the basket diagram **A** to the centre of the white fabric. Draw a second line 6mm (¼in) inside the first, then cut out the inner oval of white fabric, following the line. Snip into seam allowance and turn to wrong side along the marked line; pin, tack and press seam. Matching ovals, pin the white fabric on top of to the cream and slipstitch inner edge of oval to cream fabric. Trim the white fabric only so that it measures 26 x 36cm (10¼ x 14¼in).

8 Stitch the border Cut strips 5cm (2in) wide. Seam ends together to form two lengths 26cm (10¼in) long and two 43.5cm (17in). Press. With right sides facing take a 6mm (¼in) seam, stitch inner edges of borders to white fabric.

9 Add the quilting detail Trace the quilt motif **C** on to each corner of the cream fabric. Pin the wadding to the wrong side. Tack through all fabric layers. Using 3 strands of embroidery thread work running stitches along motif lines and inside the oval. Remove tacking stitches.

10 Finish the picture Trim off 1.5cm (⅝in) all round cream fabric and wadding. Press under 1cm (⅜in) around border edge, centre picture on calico and sew in place with straight stitch worked 6mm (¼in) from edge.

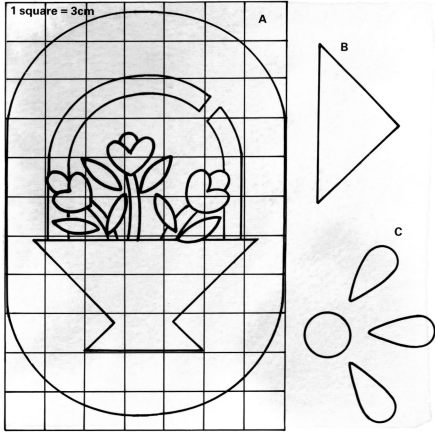

1 square = 3cm

A

B

C

Somerset patchwork

Send personal greetings to a friend with a hand-made patchwork card. A tiny piece of Somerset patchwork like this can be quickly made and fitted into a ready-made card mount. This type of patchwork requires very little stitching; it is simply made from small squares of fabric folded and pressed into triangles, producing an attractive textured surface. The first four triangles are backed with a square of calico with their points touching the centre. The next and subsequent rows then overlap each other, and are again attached to the calico backing to create the pattern.

Each patchwork piece is held on to the background square with tiny hand stitches. The whole patchwork looks especially effective as a card motif. When the patchwork is finished it is stuck to the wrong side of the card aperture and the adjoining side is folded in to cover the wrong side forming the greetings card.

Choose three different fabrics for the patchwork that mix and match together. Combine plain and prints, shiny and matt, checks and strips, whatever suits the occasion. As the design is small and purely decorative, any fabrics can be

▲ Patchwork card
This lovely patchwork card would make a perfect greeting card for a special friend.

used providing they are not too stiff or bulky. The card could even be made from small fabric pieces cut from a wedding dress or baby clothes as a memento of an anniversary.

MAKING THE CARD

Materials

Ready-made card mount 11 x 9cm (4½ x 3½in) with 6.5cm (2½in) diameter aperture

Plain cotton fabric 10 x 10cm (4 x 4in) cut on the grain, for centre patches

Cotton fabric in two different prints 20 x 10cm (8 x 4in) for second and third rows, also cut on the straight grain

Calico 10cm (4in) square for backing

Sewing thread in neutral shade

Marking pen or **pencil**

Clear adhesive

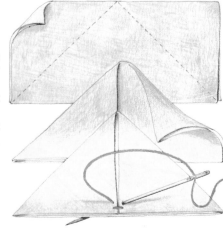

1 Cutting out the patches To form each patch, cut a 5cm (2in) square of fabric. Check that the square is cut on the straight of grain. Fold the square in half widthways with wrong sides together. Mark the centre of the raw base edges.

2 Creating triangular patches Press down each side diagonally to meet in the centre of the base, forming a triangle. Check the triangle looks even; press well. Secure with two back stitches through all thicknesses 3mm (⅛in) from the base.

3 Marking out the backing square Mark the placement lines for the patchwork on the calico. First find the centre of each side and mark across the square to divide into quarters. Finally, draw diagonal lines from corner to corner. These mark the exact positioning.

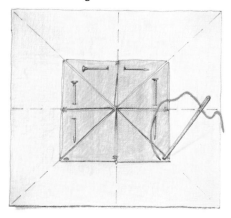
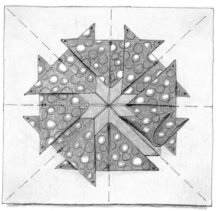
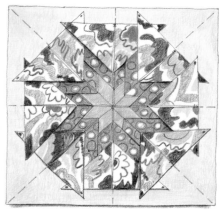

4 Place the first row Make up four triangular patches in the plain fabric, following *steps 1 and 2*. Position the triangles with points meeting in the centre; pin. Hold the patches in position by working a tiny backstitch through all layers 3mm (⅛in) in from centre base edges and at each base corner.

5 Completing the second row Make up eight triangular patches, following *steps 1 and 2*, in one of the print fabrics. Place these triangles over the first set with the centre of each triangle positioned over a marked guide line, and points 6mm (¼in) from the centre. Stitch each triangle in place as before.

6 Stitching on the third row Prepare eight patches in the second print fabric. Fix over the last row, with points 6mm (¼in) from previous row.

7 Neaten outer edge Trim down the calico backing fabric to match the patchwork and oversew the edges.

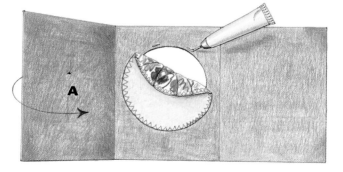

8 Mounting the patchwork Open out the card mount. Place a small amount of adhesive round the aperture on the inside of the card. Press the patchwork, right side down, centrally over the aperture. Cover the wrong side of card front (**A**) with adhesive and press over the patchwork, smoothing the card flat. Fold in the right-hand side to form the card. Write an appropriate message inside or on the card front.

Traditional patchwork

Whether a patchwork quilt is centuries old or brand new its intricate pattern always leaves you with a breathtaking admiration for the talented person who stitched it. The designs look so complicated and the stitches so tiny and neat yet, in reality, anyone who has made a patchwork knows how simple they are to make. Patience is required, because the quilts are very large and therefore take time to stitch, but most designs, including this one, are based on a square pattern made up of about a dozen patches. Once you have mastered the design of one square, you simply repeat it many times over and at the end sew them all together to make the

handsome cover. Some, like the one here also include interesting border designs which make them extra special

Once finished the patchwork is backed with a cosy wadding, quilted and lined. The quilting is not essential, but as well as looking decorative it has the practical function of holding the wadding in place.

The secret to patchwork success is really based on two simple rules. The first is to plan your design and choose your fabrics carefully before you start. This bed quilt is based on light and dark shaded fabrics in one colour. If you intend making this quilt choose colours that match your bedroom but keep to the

▲ Floral bundle
Red and white buds, polka dots, stripes and sprigs, mingle with plain reds, capturing the country spirit in this bright and breezy patchwork quilt. Note how the patchwork pieces become lost as cartwheels in the overall design.

same light and dark pattern for a similar effect. The second rule is to cut your paper patches very accurately and to tack the fabric to them carefully paying particular attention to the corners which must be sharp. The rest is child's play, you don't even need a sewing machine – it can all be stitched by hand.

PATCHWORK COVER

Materials

Patchwork fabric a selection of predominently red and white designs
Backing fabric muslin, 2m (2¼yd) square
Lining patterned fabric, colour and fibre-matched to the patchwork pieces to line the quilt, 2¼m (2½yd) square
Braid 8m (8¾ yds) each of 2.5cm (1in) and 5cm (2in) wide
Wadding hollowfill fibre, quantities same as backing fabric
Matching sewing threads red and white
Quilting thread red or white, experiment on patchwork first
Quilt needle and **hoop** to keep the fabric flat while quilting
Thin paper, pencil and **ruler** for tracing the paper patterns
Sturdy cardboard, paper glue and **craft knife**
Stiff paper old magazine covers or brown wrapping paper are ideal for cutting the paper patches

To make this delightful patchwork, which has a finished size of 2m (2¼yds) square, only a limited range of sewing techniques are required. The design has 81 squares, each consisting of 8 large and 4 small triangular patches. Nine of these squares joined together into 9 strips, make up the centre panel. Borders are added before quilting the patchwork by hand. A single bed will require 54 squares (six by nine squares).

1 Making the templates Trace the larger actual size templates (**a**, **b** and **c**) on page 31, around the black line on the pattern and glue the tracing paper shapes on the cardboard and cut out. Accuracy is essential at this stage. Repeat, for the smaller templates, (**aa**, **bb** and **cc**) tracing around the red dotted line on the pattern.

2 Cutting out the patches For each patchworked square (**x**) see below, use the template (**a**), and cut four patches in dark and four in light fabric, ensuring that fabric patterns and grains are straight. Then repeat for templates (**b**), cutting four in a different light coloured fabric. All (**b**) patches on this quilt should be cut from the same fabric to link the squares together.

3 Cutting paper patches Place templates (**aa** and **bb**) on to stiff paper and cut eight large triangles (**aa**), and four small triangles (**bb**) for each patchwork square.

4 Tacking the patches Place the paper patch (**aa**) centrally on wrong side of fabric (**a**). Fold seam allowance over and tack to form a patch. Repeat for all patches (**a** and **b**).

5 Joining patches With right sides facing, oversew one light and one dark (**a**) patch together along a long edge. Add six more alternate coloured patches to form a wheel.

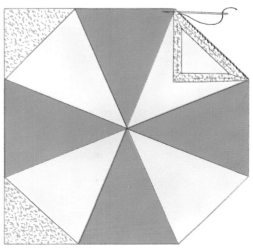

6 Forming a square Join the long sides of patches (**b**) to each light colour patch of the wheel to create a square. Repeat from *step 2* to make up 81 squares for a double quilt.

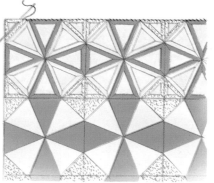

7 Joining the squares Place two squares with right sides facing and neatly oversew together, along one edge. Repeat to form nine strips of nine squares. Then place two strips together with right sides facing, pin and oversew along the long edge. Continue stitching the strips together to form the patchwork panel.

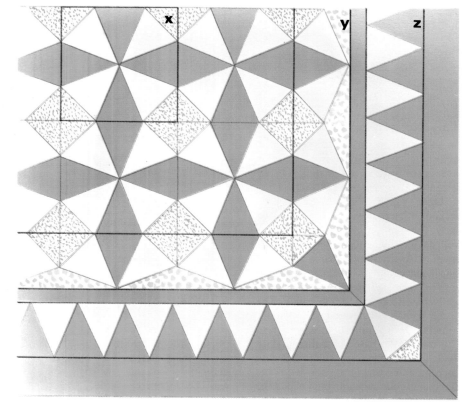

8 **Cutting out the inner border** (**y**)Following steps 2-4, cut out and make up 76 large patches (**a**) from the light fabrics and 40 from the dark fabrics, 76 small patches (**b**) cut from the same light fabric as before and 40 thin patches (**c**) all cut from the same boldly patterned light fabric.

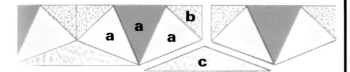

9 **Joining the border** Join three large patches (**a**) together, with the points to the centre. Alternate the colours as before, ensuring that the dark fabric is placed in the centre. Next, join a long edge of patch (**b**) to each short end of the light colour patches to make right angled corners. Repeat to make 36 of these panels. Join nine panels by stitching the short sides of the thin patches (**c**) to the long edges of patches (**a**). Then stitch the small patches (**b**) together forming the strips, as shown. Repeat, to make three more strips.

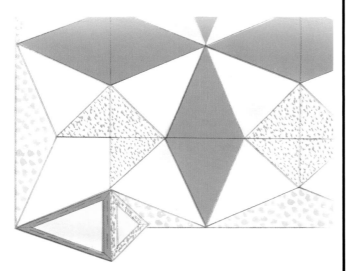

10 **Adding the border** With right sides facing, handstitch the border strips (**y**) along the four sides of the patchwork square as before. To finish each corner, join a small patch (**b**) and a large dark patch (**a**) together to form a kite shape. Repeat to make four kite shapes and then stitch one to each corner, filling the voids between the border strips and creating a square again.

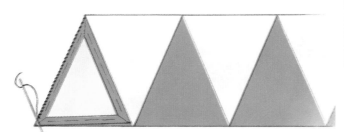

11 **Forming the outer border** (**z**) This border is made from four strips, to attach to each side of the quilt. Cut out and make up 52 large patches (**a**), 26 in light fabrics and 26 in dark fabrics. With right sides facing, sew the patches together making a straight sided strip, alternating the light and dark patches. Repeat from step 11 to create three more strips, beginning and ending each with a dark patch. Finally, sew one light coloured patch (**a** and **b**) to each corner of the outer border.

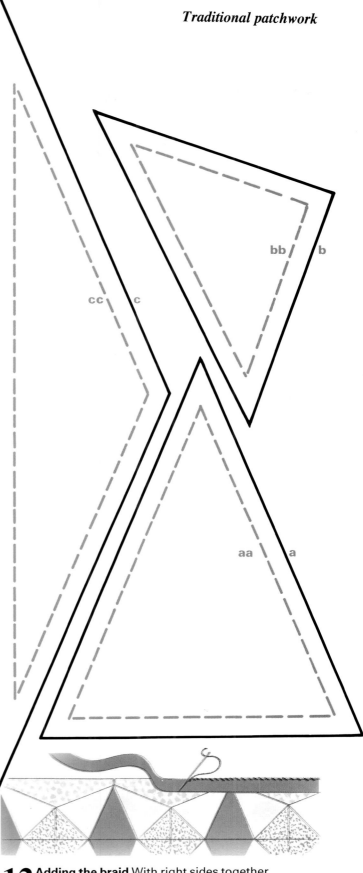

12 **Adding the braid** With right sides together, oversew the 2.5cm (1in) braid around the sides of the patchwork panel, neatly mitring the braid at the corners. Then oversew the outer patchwork border (**z**) to the braid in the same way, taking care to match corners.

13 **Removing paper patches** Finally, remove the tacking stitches and the paper patches from the patchwork. Press the patchwork in preparation for the quilting and open out the raw edges.

QUILTING AND LINING THE COVER

The patchwork is now ready for quilting and making up into a bed quilt. The quilting lines, are simply handstitched, 5mm (¼in) from and parallel to the sides of the patches, adding a truly nostalgic touch to the quilt. Quilting is not altogether necessary and should you wish to, you can eliminate this step and proceed to line the patchwork at this stage.

1 Adding the wadding Lay the backing fabric on to a flat surface and place the wadding and then the patchwork with right sides facing upward on top. Pin and tack together around and across the panel, sandwiching the wadding between the two fabrics.

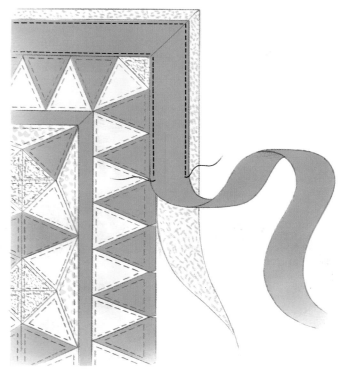

2 Using the quilting hoop Place a part of the patchwork in the quilting hoop and using the quilting thread and needle, sew tiny quilting stitches 5mm (¼in) from the edge of each patch. Ensure the stitches and spaces are even in length and as discreet as possible. Also ensure that they are always the same 5mm (¼in) distance from the patchwork seams. Move the quilting hoop around the patchwork until the whole area is quilted.

3 Lining the quilt Trim the wadding to fit the patchwork and place centrally over the lining fabric, with wrong sides facing. Then pin and tack together all round. Fold the excess fabric of the lining to the right side butting up to the edges of the quilt and pin and tack in place. Turn in the corners to create a mitred effect, then place the 5cm (2in) braid centrally over the raw edges and covering the patch seam allowance, pin and top stitch in place all round the quilt.

▼ Optical illusion
The finished quilt transforms the triangles into a kaleidoscope of different shapes and patterns each time you look; red stars on a white background; expanding cartwheels; spiralling circles and white diamonds swirl in and out of prominence.

Patchwork bed-quilt Part 1

The origins of quilt-making lie more in down-to-earth practicalities than in a quest for style and decorative effects. Warmth and durability were the key factors on the quilter's mind, and patchwork was simply a constructive way to make use of leftover scraps of fabric. Today, however, quilts are appreciated as much, if not more, for their beauty and charm, as for their usefulness, and quilt-making is undergoing a huge resurgence in popularity.

The stunning quilt featured here is made up from a total of 21 panels, some of which are square and some rectangular. Each panel is individually worked before being joined to its neighbours by means of a network of fine border strips. Some of the panels are made up from colourful patchwork shapes, while others are prettily quilted and appliquéd with a range of motifs. You can keep to the appliqué motifs given here, or choose a few of your own to create a more personalised quilt.

Traditional blue and cream fabrics, with a hint of red, have been used to make up this quilt, which looks intricate without appearing fussy. When choosing the fabrics for your quilt, try to restrict yourself to using only two or three colours – this will be sufficient to create a bright quilt, while still allowing the intricacies of the design to be fully appreciated. If you find it difficult to envisage the finished result, draw your own colour chart like the one shown on page 34, using pencils in shades as close to your fabrics as possible. This will give you an idea of the finished look.

Make sure that all the fabrics used in the quilt, including the appliquéd motifs, patchwork shapes and the lining, are similar in weight, weave and care

▲ Family heirloom
Combine the traditional skills of decorative quilting, patchwork and appliqué to create this magnificent heirloom quilt, which your family will cherish for years to come. Use shades of cream and blue, as here, or select colours of your own, but keep to subtle, delicate prints for the best results.

qualities. Wash all the fabrics before you begin, to check for colour-fastness and shrinkage, then press them to remove any creases. The finished size of the quilt is 219cm (92in) square.

Pages 34–38 give details on how to stitch the square panels at the centre of the quilt and at each corner. Instructions for stitching the remaining rectangular panels, and for making up and lining the quilt follow on pages 39–42.

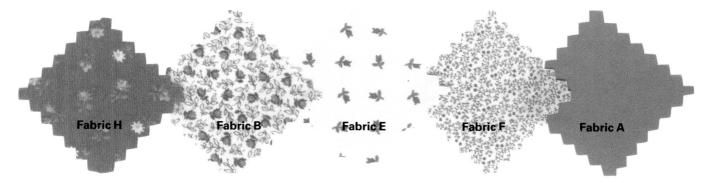

Fabric H   Fabric B   Fabric E   Fabric F   Fabric A

Materials

Note: All the fabric quantities given are based on a fabric width of 120cm (47¼in). Work from one set of measurements only.

Plain blue fabric (A), 3m (3¾yds)
Blue fabric with bold pattern (B), 120cm (4ft)
Striped blue fabric or ticking (C), 40cm (16in)
Plain cream fabric (D), 2m (3¼yds)
Cream fabric with pattern (E), 120cm (4ft)

Blue fabric with subtle pattern (F), 230cm (3yds)
Plain red fabric (G), 30cm (1ft)
Blue, red and cream patterned fabric (H), 40cm (16in)
Backing fabric, 5m (6½yds); use good quality muslin or a similar fine cotton
Cream lining fabric, 4.5m (5½yds)
2cm (¾in) thick wadding, 8m (9yds) of 90cm (35½in) wide wadding; cotton wadding is traditionally used, but polyester is also suitable (remember to dry-clean the quilt if using cotton)

Iron-on interfacing, 50cm (20in)
Quilting bar (optional)
Stiff card to make the patchwork and appliqué templates
Paper to make paper linings for the patches; use old greetings cards or the stiff covers from glossy magazines
Sharp scissors Ideally you should have two pairs – one for cutting paper and one for fabric
Craft knife for cutting the stiff card
Matching sewing threads
Needles and **pins**

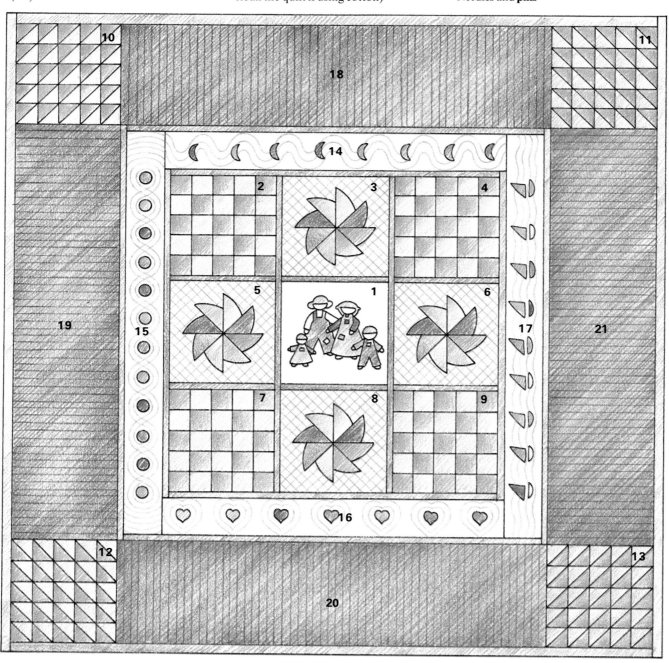

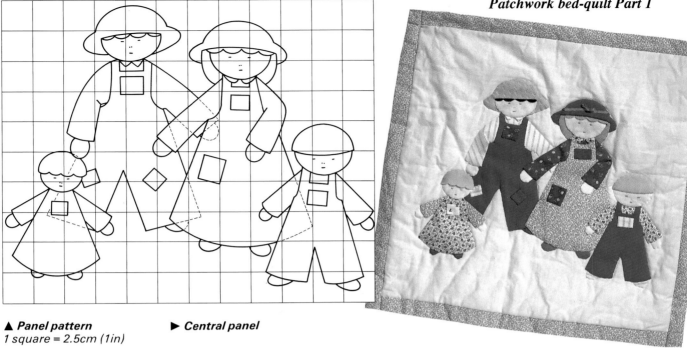

▲ **Panel pattern**
1 square = 2.5cm (1in)

► **Central panel**

CENTRAL APPLIQUE PANEL

The central panel of the quilt (Panel 1 on the colour chart) is ideal for personalising your work with appliquéd motifs of your choice. Whether you choose an elaborate design, like the family portrait featured here, or far simpler motifs, the results will be just as charming and individual. This panel is left unquilted to give full emphasis to the appliquéd design.

1 **Preparing the panel** Cut a 40cm (17in) square from plain cream fabric (Fabric D), and one of both backing fabric and wadding to same size; cut along straight grain of fabric. Sandwich the wadding between the two fabrics, with the fabrics right side out; pin and tack together vertically and horizontally through all layers, every 10cm (4in).

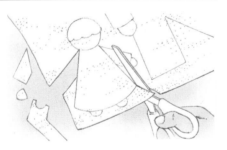

2 **Cutting out** Draw your chosen motifs on to paper, keeping the outlines simple. Once happy with your design, trace the motifs on to iron-on interfacing and carefully cut out. If using the family portrait given here, first enlarge it on a grid – one square = 2.5cm (1in). Then trace the figures on to interfacing, spacing them out. Cut out each component, such as arms, head and clothes, separately, as these will be made up from different fabrics.

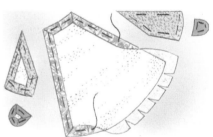

3 **Tacking round the motifs** Iron each part of your design in place on the back of your chosen appliqué fabrics. Cut around each shape, leaving a 5mm (¼in) border. Snip into the border around curves and corners, to help fabric lie flat when turned under. Neatly fold the border to the wrong side, taking the edge of the interfacing as your guide, and tack in place. Cut out any details, like pockets and patches, from fabric scraps and appliqué in place.

4 **Securing the motifs** Centre your design over the cream fabric of your tacked panel, carefully positioning each component and overlapping the parts where necessary; pin in place. Use matching sewing thread to slipstitch around the edges of each motif, starting with the largest, underlying ones. Remove tacking from motifs.

tip

Embroidered details
Embroider decorative details, like the family figures' eyes and mouths, on to your motifs before stitching them in place.

Suitable fabrics
To make the quilt, use closely woven fabrics which will provide a firm background for the appliqué, but make sure they are soft enough to be easily manageable and to give a good finish when quilted. Keep to natural fabrics which are more in keeping with the traditional style of the quilt, and are available in a wide range of mini-prints. Lightweight cottons are ideal and not too expensive; fine linen, lawn, lightweight wool and wool/cotton mixtures will also work well.

PATCHWORK SQUARES

The central panel is bordered with four colourful panels of patchwork (Panels 2, 4, 7 and 9 on the colour chart on page 34), each one consisting of small square patches, made up from two contrasting fabrics.

1 Making the templates On stiff card, draw two squares, one 8.5cm (3¾in) and one 7cm (3in). Cut out the squares with a craft knife. Accuracy is vital at this stage, so double-check your measurements, and make sure all edges are straight and all angles right angles.

▼ *Sweet dreams*
The quilt is displayed to perfection on a sturdy wooden bedstead, bringing a welcome burst of colour and pattern into this otherwise simple bedroom.

2 Marking up patches Draw around the smaller square templates on stiff paper, to mark up a total of 100 squares, and cut out. Take the blue fabric with bold pattern (Fabric B) and mark 52 squares on it, drawing around the larger square template; line up the edges of the square with the straight grain of the fabric. Repeat to mark up 48 squares on the patterned cream fabric (Fabric E). Carefully cut out all squares.

3 Tacking the patches Centre a paper square over the wrong side of each patch and anchor with a pin. Fold the narrow side borders over to the back of each patch, overlapping the corners neatly, and tack in place through all layers. Remove pins and press with an iron.

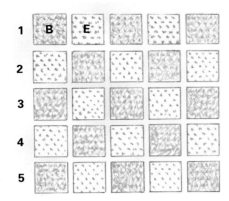

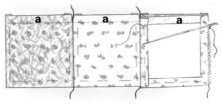

6 Forming the panels Take the top two strips of each panel and put right sides together and edges matching. Oversew along the long edge to join the two, removing tacking stitches from outer side borders and opening borders out before stitching to end. Repeat to attach other three strips.

4 Arranging the patches Divide the patches into four sets of 25, each set containing 12 patches in Fabric E and 13 patches in Fabric B. Arrange each set into a square panel as shown, alternating colours to create a chequered effect; make sure each corner patch is in Fabric B.

5 Joining the patches Take the first two patches at top of one panel and put right sides facing and edges matching. Oversew along side edge to join the two patches, stitching through fabric only; stop stitching just before you reach top edge, remove tacking stitches holding top border in place, and open border out (**a**); this border needs to be opened out on all outer edges of panel, to create a seam allowance. Repeat to join on next three patches. Make up four more strips, opening out border along bottom edge of last strip.

7 Removing the papers Remove tacking stitches and paper templates, trying not to tear templates which can be re-used for the patchwork triangles. Check that seam allowance hangs freely.

8 Adding the wadding Cut out four squares of wadding and of backing fabric to same size as patchwork panels. Sandwich each square of wadding between a patchwork panel and backing fabric; tack together.

PATCHWORK TRIANGLES

The four outer corners of the quilt are highlighted with four more patchwork panels (Panels 10, 11, 12 and 13 on the chart), made up from triangular patches in two fabrics to match the patchwork square panels.

1 Making a triangular template The patchwork triangles on these panels are exactly half the size of the patchwork squares, so to make the triangular template, simply draw a diagonal line across the larger square template. Cut in half to give two triangles 8.5 x 8.5 x 12cm (3¾ x 3¾ x 5¼in). If the original square template is a bit battered, make a new one to cut in half.

2 Making paper linings No template is necessary for the paper linings – simply cut your square patchwork papers in half, as for the card templates, to give triangles 7 x 7 x 10cm (3 x 3 x 4¼in). If some of the original papers have been torn, mark up and cut out more 7cm (3in) squares to cut in half. You will need 200 stiff paper triangles in total.

3 Cutting out Take the blue fabric with bold pattern (Fabric B) and the patterned cream fabric (Fabric E), and draw around the triangular template to mark up a total of 100 triangles on each fabric; line up the short sides of the triangles with the straight grain of the fabric. Cut out carefully.

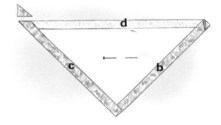

4 Tacking the patches Centre a paper triangle over the wrong side of each patch and anchor with a pin. Fold one short side border (**b**), and then the other (**c**) back over the paper lining, neatly folding corner. Trim pointed tips of side borders. Then fold in the sharply angled corners as shown, before folding back long border edge (**d**). Tack in place and remove pin. Press patches.

5 Making up the panels Take two tacked patches, one of each fabric, and put them right sides together and edges matching. Oversew the two together along their long edge to make a square when opened out. Repeat with all the other patches. Sew the squares together to make strips of five, alternating the colours as shown.

Then sew sets of five strips together to make up four square panels in total; be sure to leave the outer side hems around each panel unstitched to create a seam allowance, as you did for the patchwork square panels.

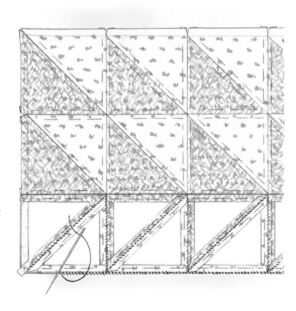

6 Adding the wadding Remove all the tacking stitches and take out the paper linings. Cut out four squares of wadding and of backing fabric to the same size as the patchwork panels, ie 35cm (15in) plus seam allowances. Tack wadding and backing fabric to the panels as for *Patchwork square panels* on page 36.

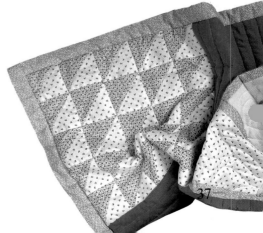

STAR PANELS

Four quilted squares of cream fabric (Panels 3, 5, 6 and 8 on the chart) border the central panel, each one appliquéd with a multicoloured 'star' motif. Use a mixture of your quilt fabrics to make up each star, or introduce some new, co-ordinating ones to add a little more variety.

1 Cutting out Cut four 40cm (17in) squares from the plain cream fabric (Fabric D), and four of both the backing fabric and the wadding to same size; cut fabric out along the straight grain. Sandwich each square of wadding between a main fabric and a backing fabric square, right sides out; tack together horizontally and vertically, every 10cm (4in)

2 Quilting the panel Use tailor's chalk to mark up the two diagonals on the cream top fabric, and machine stitch along them. Set quilting bar to 2.5cm (1in), then stitch diagonally across the panel in one direction, starting at centre and working out to corners; swing the panel round and quilt on the diagonal in the other direction to form a trellis pattern. If you do not have a quilting bar, mark up the pattern with tailor's chalk and a ruler before stitching. Remove tacking stitches.

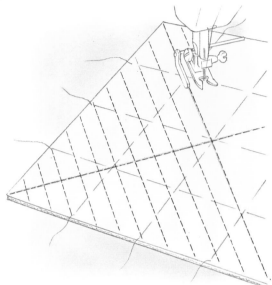

3 Marking up the star motifs Enlarge then trace off the large and small triangular shapes for the star on to stiff card. Cut out with a craft knife to make templates. Draw around the small template to mark up 32 shapes on stiff paper and cut out. Use the large template to mark up 32 shapes on the wrong side of a selection of your various quilt fabrics, and cut out.

4 Tacking the star motifs Centre a paper shape over the wrong side of each fabric shape, and hold in place with a pin. Fold the narrow borders over to the back of the fabric, neatly overlapping all the corners; snip into the border along the curved edge to help the fabric lie flat. Tack the borders in place, remove the pins and press.

5 Forming the stars Divide your 32 shapes into sets of eight, each set containing a range of fabrics. Arrange each set into a star as shown. Join shapes by placing two together, right sides facing and centre points (**p**) together, so that the short straight edges lie against the long straight edges; oversew together along one edge.

Join shapes 1, 2, 3 and 4 first, followed by shapes 5, 6, 7 and 8. Finish by placing the two halves of each star right sides together, and oversew down the middle to join the two.

6 Stitching the stars in place Centre each star over the top of a quilted square, and pin securely in place. Sew around the edges of the star with tiny slipstitches. Before sewing down the last curve, remove all the tacking stitches and carefully pull out the paper linings.

Quick results for patchwork
The instructions given here are for traditional, hand-sewn patchwork, but if short of time, you can easily do away with the paper linings and simply machine stitch the patches together. (For details on machine stitching both square and triangular patches, see page 18.

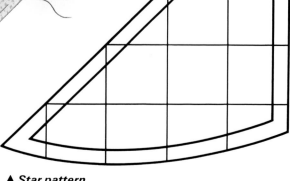

▲ **Star pattern**
1 square = 2.5cm (1in)

Once you have completed the central patchwork and appliqué panels of the quilt, together with the four corner panels, you will find the remaining rectangular pieces relatively fast to make up. The long, slim outer panels are simply quilted across their width with evenly spaced rows of stitching, while the smaller panels surrounding the central squares are quilted with a range of different designs. These more intricate quilting patterns follow the outlines of the various colourful motifs with which the smaller rectangular panels are decorated, adding movement and texture to the surface of the quilt.

When all the panels have been made up and trimmed to size, they are joined together with a network of slim border strips, starting with the smaller central panels, and working out to the larger outer ones. As well as joining all the pieces together, the borders create a pretty frame for each panel, clearly defining each section so that it can be appreciated individually, as well as a part of the quilt as a whole. Stitching the panels together is one of the most satisfying elements of making a quilt, as you watch all your work take shape and

▲ A flair for design
When all the panels have been joined, you can appreciate the full impact of the design. The fabrics are carefully positioned to create a perfect balance of colour.

quickly come to fruition.

The quilt is lined to enclose all the raw edges, and trimmed with a matching border, slightly wider than the strips linking the panels together.

For the numbering of panels used here, please refer to the colour chart on page 34.

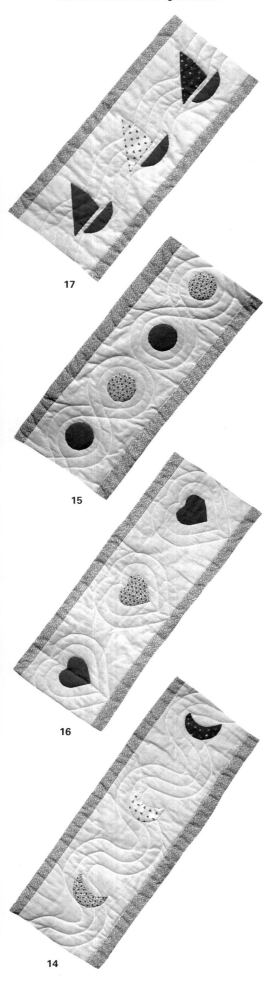

17

15

16

14

CREAM BORDER PANELS

These long, slim border panels (Panels 14, 15, 16 and 17 on the colour chart) are quilted with a variety of designs, before being appliquéd with simple motifs in a range of colourful fabrics.

1 Cutting out the panels Cut two 150 x 20cm (62½ x 7in) rectangles of plain cream fabric (Fabric D), together with two of backing fabric and two of wadding to the same size. Also cut two 125 x 20cm (52½ x 7in) rectangles of the cream fabric, with two of backing fabric and two of wadding to the same size; these measurements include seam allowances and allow for 'shrinkage' during quilting. For each panel, sandwich the wadding between the two fabrics, right sides out, and pin and tack together every 15cm (6in).

2 Making the templates Enlarge each of the motif shapes given overleaf (ie the heart, the moon, and the boat sail and hull) – each square = 12mm (½in). Trace off the outlines on to stiff card, and cut out carefully to make a template for each one. Also draw a circle on to stiff card, 4cm (1½in) in diameter, for the sun motifs; cut out carefully.

3 Cutting out the motifs Draw around the templates to mark each motif on to iron-on interfacing; you will need eight suns, eight boat sails and hulls, seven moons and seven hearts. Cut out the shapes. Iron each one in place on the back of a selection of your quilt fabrics (and on other co-ordinating fabrics if you wish, for added variety); make sure the fabric pattern is attractively positioned on each motif. Cut out the motifs, allowing a 5mm (¼in) fabric border all round for turning under.

4 Tacking the motifs On each motif, snip into the fabric border around curves and points, so that the fabric will lie flat when turned under. Then neatly fold the border to the wrong side, taking the edge of the interfacing as your guide; tack in place through all layers.

5 Marking motifs' positions Mark up the positions of the heart and the moon motifs on the shorter cream quilted panels, spacing them out to lie an equal distance apart. Repeat for the sun and the boat motifs on the longer cream quilted panels; use a dressmaker's marking pen to mark up the outline of each motif on the panel, by lightly drawing around the card template. This will serve as a guide for the quilted patterns.

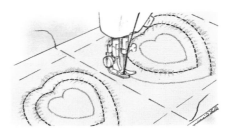

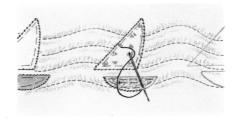

6 Quilting the panels Use tailor's chalk to lightly mark up the quilting design on each panel – ie wavy lines on the moon and boat panels, and motif outlines on the heart and sun panels. Arrange the quilted lines to curve decoratively around or over the chalked outlines of your motifs, and space the lines 2cm (¾in) apart. Quilt the design, then remove all the tacking stitches. If preferred, the panels can be quilted with straight lines along their length.

7 Attaching the motifs Pin the motifs in place on each panel, taking the chalked outlines as your guide. Slipstitch around each one to attach it to the panel. Remove the pins and tacking stitches from the motifs.

BLUE BORDER PANELS

Four plain blue quilted rectangles (Panels 18, 19, 20 and 21 on the chart) form the quilt's outer border.

1 Cutting out panels Cut out four 155 x 37cm (64 x 15 ¾in) rectangles of plain blue fabric (Fabric A), together with four of wadding and four of backing fabric. For each panel, pin and tack the fabric and wadding together as for the Cream border panels.

2 Quilting the panels Quilt a series of straight lines across the width of each panel, spacing the lines 2.5cm (1in) apart. Remove the tacking stitches from the panels.

Using fabric remnants
Any leftover scraps of fabric can be used to make colourful patchwork cushion covers to match the quilt.

MAKING UP THE QUILT

Note that all the square panels have a 7mm (¼in) seam allowance all round, while the rectangular panels and border strips have a slightly larger allowance of 1cm (⅜in). You should therefore make adjustments as necessary when joining the panels, making sure that all the border strips are 2cm (¾in) wide when stitched in place, and that all the seams are aligned at corners.

1 Trimming central panels Take the central square panels (Panels 1-9 on the chart) and lay them out flat. Trim the central panel and the star panels to exactly the same size as your patchwork square panels – ie to 35cm (15in) square, plus a 7mm (¼in) seam allowance all round.

2 Trimming outer panels Trim the two short cream rectangular panels (Panels 14 and 16) to measure 115 x 15cm (48¾ x 5¾in). Repeat for the longer cream rectangular panels (Panels 15 and 17) to measure 141 x 15cm (58¾ x 5¾in). Finally, trim the blue rectangular panels (Panels 18, 19, 20 and 21) to 145 x 37cm (60¼ x 15¾in). All these measurements include a 1cm (⅜in) seam allowance.

3 Cutting out border strips From the subtly patterned blue fabric (F), cut slim border strips 4cm (1½in) wide and to the following lengths: six 37cm (15¾in) long, four 111cm (47¼in) long, two 115cm (48¾in) long, two 141cm (58¾in) long, and two 145cm (60¼in) long. Cut out along the straight grain. Also cut and make up four strips 221 x 5cm (92¾ x 2in) for the quilt's outer edges.

4 Attaching short strips Lay the central panel (Panel 1) out flat, right side up. Take one of the very short border strips and lay it along the top edge of the panel, with right sides together and long edges matching. Pin, tack and stitch the strip in place, taking the recommended seam allowances.

5 Joining central panels Open out the border to lie right side up. Place an appliquéd star panel (Panel 3) over it, with right sides facing and the edge of the star panel lined up with the top edge of the border strip. Pin, tack and stitch the strip to the star panel, taking the recommended seam allowances as before. Repeat to join a second star panel (Panel 8) to the bottom edge of Panel 1, with another short border strip. Use short border strips to join together Panels 2, 5 and 7, and Panels 4, 6 and 9 in the same way.

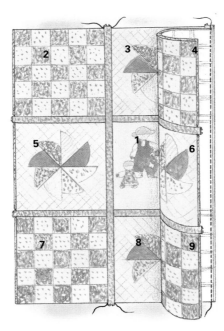

6 Joining strips of panels Lie the central strip of panels (Panels 3, 1 and 8) out flat, with right side up. Place one 111cm (47¼in) border strip over both long side edges of these panels, with right sides together and edges matching. Pin, tack and stitch the strips in place, taking the recommended seam allowances; make sure these vertical border strips lie at a perfect right angle to the short horizontal border strips. Open out the borders, and stitch them to the two neighbouring strips of panels as shown, thus linking all the central panels together

7 Bordering central panels Join the two remaining 111cm (47¼in) border strips to the top and bottom of this central group of panels, by putting right sides together and matching edges as before. Open out the borders. Then stitch the two 115cm (48¾in) border strips to both side edges of the group of panels in the same way. As you stitch the strips in place, keep checking that they lie perfectly straight across the panels, and form right angles with other strips.

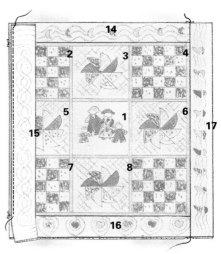

8 Attaching outer panels Stitch Panels 14 and 16 in place along the top and bottom edges of the central group of panels, attaching them to the border strips as before. Repeat to attach Panels 15 and 17 to the side border strips around the central group of panels; where the border strip stops, simply continue stitching these panels to the short ends of Panels 14 and 16, as shown.

9 Adding border strips Stitch one 141cm (58¾in) border strip across the top edge of Panel 14 and across the ends of Panels 15 and 17. Repeat to attach the second 141cm (58¾in) strip to the bottom edge of Panel 16. Stitch the 145cm (60¼in) border strips to the outer edges of Panels 15 and 17. Then stitch two of the quilted blue border panels (Panels 18 and 20) in place along the top and bottom border strips.

10 Attaching blue outer panels Lay out one of the remaining quilted blue border panels with right side up. Lie one of the patchwork triangle panels over it at each end, with right sides facing and edges matching. Stitch together across the short edges of the blue panel, taking the recommended seam allowances. Repeat on other blue border panel. Stitch these panels (Panels 10, 19 and 12, and Panels 11, 21 and 13) in place on both sides of the quilt, attaching them to the border strips and to the side edges of the other two quilted blue panels (Panels 18 and 20).

11 Pressing seam allowances Once you have assembled the quilt, lay it out flat with wrong side up. Press all the seam allowances on each side of the border strips inwards, to lie behind the strips rather than behind the fabric panels. The border strips will then be padded out to the same thickness as the panels, giving the quilt an even finish.

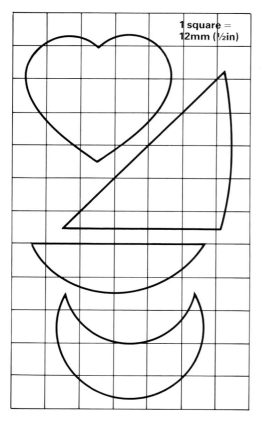

1 square =
12mm (½in)

LINING THE QUILT

1 Attaching border strips Lay the quilt out flat with right side up. Take one of the 221 x 5cm (92 ¾ x 2in) border strips and place it over the top edge of the quilt, with long edges matching and right sides together; pin, tack and stitch in place, taking a 1cm (⅜in) seam allowance. Repeat on the bottom edge of the quilt, then open out both border strips to lie right side up.

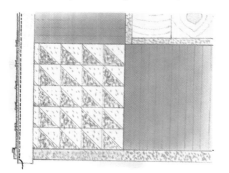

2 Stitching the corners Take a third outer border strip and place it over one of the unstitched edges of the quilt, with right sides facing and edges matching. Taking a 1cm (⅜in) seam allowance, pin, tack and stitch in place, stitching across the neighbouring border strips at each corner, right to the end. Repeat to attach fourth border strip to the opposite edge. Trim away the ends of the top and bottom borders to lie flush with fabric edge. Open out the border strips to lie right side up.

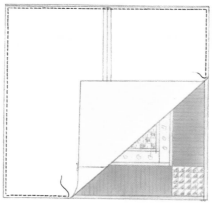

3 Making the lining Join widths of your lining fabric to make up a 221cm (92 ¾in) square of fabric. Place the lining over the quilt, with right sides together and the lining edges matching the edges of the border strips. Pin, tack and stitch together around edges, taking a 1cm (⅜in) seam allowance and leaving an opening across one edge for turning through to the right side.

▲ The key to success
The quilt featured here successfully combines a multitude of different fabrics, appliquéd motifs, patchwork shapes and quilting patterns, in a wonderfully harmonious design. Use subtly patterned fabrics in two or three shades for the best results.

tip

A well-defined border
If you find that the lining fabric slips forward to the front of your finished quilt, hold the quilt's outer border firmly in place by topstitching around its inner edge.

4 Stitching the opening Turn the quilt through to the right side. Fold in the raw edges across the opening and slipstitch closed.

Easy-to-sew quilts

Traditional, hand-stitched patch-work is an immensely satisfying pastime, and provides a wonderful opportunity to use up fabric scraps and remnants creatively. Whether making a large project, like one of the quilts featured here, or a smaller one, such as a cushion, you can watch your work quickly grow with each patch you add.

In traditional patchwork, the same shape is used throughout the quilt, with the most popular choices being squares, triangles, diamonds and hexagons. Once you have decided on the patch shape, a wide variety of exciting designs can be created by combining plain and pat-terned fabric patches in different ways.

The simplest way to work a quilt is to develop a basic patchwork design from a block of patches, such as a diamond shape, or a patchwork flower. This design is then repeated over and over, using the same or different fabrics each time, depending on the desired effect. Once completed, the blocks of patches are joined together, either directly or by means of intermediary patches in a toning 'background' fabric – usually white or cream.

Lightweight, printed and plain dress cottons are most commonly used for patchwork, but many other fabrics can also be used to good effect. The main criterion to bear in mind is that all your fabrics must be of similar weight, weave and durability, and have the same care properties. Wash the fabrics before cutting to check for colour fastness and shrinkage, and press to remove creases.

▼ Personalised patchwork
This charming quilt design is created entirely from square patches in shades of blue, pink, red and cream. At the centre of each patchwork diamond lie the signatures of friends and relatives, lovingly embroidered by the quilt maker.

HEXAGONAL PATCHWORK

Materials

Selection of fabrics for the patches, including a good supply of cream-coloured fabric for the 'background' patches; fabric quantities will depend on the size of the quilt

Mediumweight wadding

Lining fabric

Plastic or metal, hexagonal window template, available from haberdashery departments and specialist shops

Isometric paper This is paper printed with triangles, and is ideal for marking up hexagonal patchwork designs; it is available from art and graphic supply shops and some stationers

Stiff paper to make the paper linings for the patches; use old greetings cards or stiff pages cut from glossy magazines

Scissors You should have one pair for cutting paper, and a separate pair for cutting fabric

Matching sewing threads

Tailor's chalk and **sharp pins**

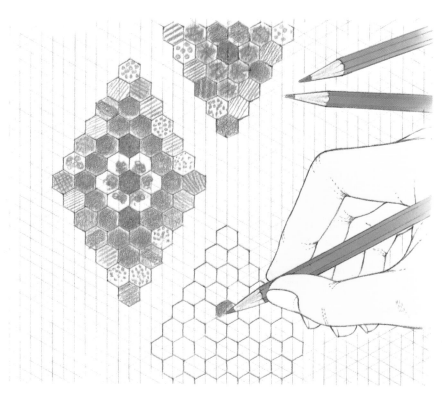

The quilt featured here is made up entirely from hexagonal patches. A range of colourful patches are hand stitched together to form large patchwork diamonds, which are then joined with a network of cream-coloured patches to form the quilt. Each diamond contains a total of 49 patches. The quilt is lightly padded with mediumweight wadding and lined. These instructions can easily be adapted for making up a quilt using patches of a different shape. Simply plan your design with care before you begin, as described in step 1.

1 Planning the quilt Once you have decided on a basic design for the quilt – in this case, a diamond pattern – plan the colour arrangement on isometric paper, using coloured pencils to match your fabrics. Aim for a good balance of colour throughout, so that plain, pale fabrics are offset by stronger colours and patterns. To unify the overall design, create a focal point at the centre of each patchwork diamond by using patches of the same, strong colour, like the bright red patches used here. Shade in half-diamonds around the quilt's edges.

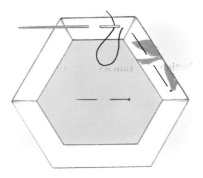

2 Cutting out patches

Draw around the outside of the window template with a dressmaker's marking pen, to mark up hexagons on the right side of your fabrics. Move the template around to find the best pattern arrangement where necessary; here, floral motifs are placed along one edge of the template window, rather than centred, so they will fan out from the central patch when stitched in place around it. Always line up two of the straight sides of the template with the straight grain of the fabric. Carefully cut out all the patches and put each set in a separate plastic bag, to avoid mixing them up. Use your plan to see how many patches you need.

3 Tacking the patches

Mark up and cut out a supply of stiff paper linings, drawing around the inside of the window template. Centre a paper lining over the wrong side of each patch, and anchor with a pin. Working your way around each patch, fold the narrow side borders over to the back and tack them in place through all layers; neatly overlap each corner. Remove the pins and press the patches with an iron. Keep the patches in their separate bags as you work.

4 Arranging the patches

Divide the coloured patches into groups of 49, and arrange each group into a diamond shape, referring to your colour plan. Surround each diamond and half-diamond with a row of cream patches to link them all together, and fill in the gaps with more cream patches. Add an extra row of cream patches around the quilt's edges.

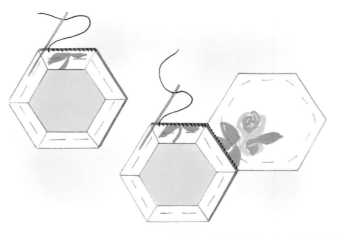

5 Joining patches

Stand back to check the effect, and move patches around until happy with the colour arrangement. Join the patches in each diamond and half-diamond by placing them right sides facing and edges matching, and oversewing along their edges. Start at the diamond's centre, and work outwards. Match all corner points and strengthen with two or three extra stitches.

6 Assembling the quilt

Stitch the cream patches in place around the diamonds and half-diamonds. Then join all the patchwork sections together, placing them right sides facing and oversewing along the edges. Work out from the quilt's centre, adding in the extra cream patches between the diamond points and finishing with the border patches along the outside edges. Remove tacking stitches and templates, and press.

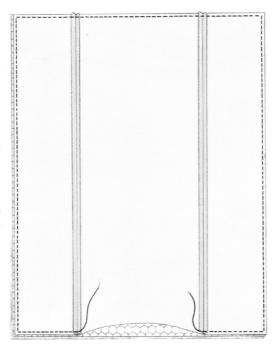

◄ **Patchwork diamonds**
The patches on this quilt have been stitched to form diamonds. Create other designs by altering the arrangement of patches.

7 Lining the quilt

Join widths of wadding and of lining fabric to make up a single piece of each, the same size as the patchwork quilt. Sandwich the quilt between the wadding and the lining, with right sides facing and edges matching. Stitch all three layers together, taking a 1.5cm (⅝in) seam allowance and leaving an opening in one edge. Trim the corners and any overhanging half-hexagons, then turn the quilt through to the right side. Slipstich across the opening.

tip

Anchoring the layers
To stop the quilt layers slipping, anchor them together with a few tiny stitches at intervals across the quilt.

QUICK PATCHWORK

For really quick results, you can simply machine stitch together fabric rectangles and squares of all sizes, to create a quilt with a wonderfully authentic patchwork feel. To make this quilt, use similar fabrics as for the hexagonal patchwork quilt.

1 Cutting out Lay your selection of fabrics out flat, with right sides up. Using a long ruler and a set square, mark up squares and rectangles on the fabrics with tailor's chalk. Make sure you mark up along the straight grain. On each fabric, mark up groups of patches to four or five fixed widths, so that when you come to make up the quilt, patches of the same width can easily be joined together to form neat strips. Carefully cut out all the patches with a sharp pair of scissors.

2 Arranging the patches Clear a large empty space on the floor and arrange the patches into strips, matching edges of the same width or length. Each strip should equal the finished width of the quilt, plus seam allowances for joining patches. When all the patches are in place, step back to check the effect; move patches around as necessary to achieve a good balance of colour.

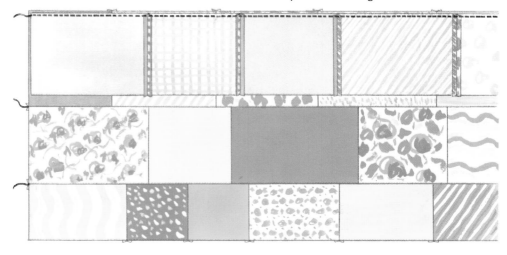

3 Making up the quilt Working on one strip at a time, join the patches together by putting them right sides facing and stitching along the appropriate edge. Press the seam allowances open. Then join the strips of patches in the same way to make up the quilt, and press the seam allowances open as before. If necessary, trim the edges of the quilt so they are straight.

Seam together widths of wadding and of lining fabric, to make up one piece of each to the same size as the quilt. Stitch the three layers together to line the quilt, as for the *Hexagonal patchwork quilt.*

◄ *Patches of all sizes*
By varying the size of the patches, you can create a quilt with a wonderfully haphazard appearance, and a genuine patchwork feel. All the patches are simply machine stitched together, so your work will quickly come to fruition. Use fabric scraps and remnants in all the colours of the rainbow, and mix and match them as much as you please.

Heirloom quilt

This traditional hand-made quilt is sure to inspire you into action. Once completed, it will become a treasured heirloom to be passed down through generations of your family. Featuring a range of crafts, such as patchwork, appliqué and quilting, all of which combine to provide an interesting mix of texture and design, the quilt will be valued for its richness and detail.

The addition of coloured fabric motifs provides interest and composition to what would otherwise be a plain white quilt. Each patchwork piece is cleverly designed to interlock, creating the

stately twin-handled urn, which is then topped with a delightful array of appliqué flowers and birds.

Make the quilt even more memorable by reviving old fabrics for which you have fond memories and associations, giving them a new lease of life as patchwork or appliqué details – an old cushion or favourite chair cover, perhaps. Wash all the fabric pieces before you begin, to check for shrinkage and colour fastness. The areas between the motifs offer the perfect backdrop to display the beautiful quilting details, adding to the diversity of the piece.

▲ Summer quilt
Whether this delightful quilt is used for a chair throw or a bed, it is sure to make an impact. The quilt is made up from a mixture of square and triangular shapes, sewn together to make a truly traditional patchwork cover. It is then machine quilted with various different designs and adorned with charming bird and flower appliqué shapes.

MAKING THE QUILT

Materials

Main fabric in white cotton for the main quilt area and the lining, 3.4m (3⅝yds) long and 135cm (54in) wide
Co-ordinating patchwork pieces in a variety of colour-fast printed fabrics for the patchwork urns and appliqué flowers
Heavyweight wadding hollow-fill fibre, 128 x 168cm (51 x 67in)
Matching sewing threads
Cardboard, quality magazine paper, tailor's chalk and **scissors** to make the templates
White quilting thread, needle and **hoop** to quilt the cover

This traditional quilt is made predominantly from triangular and diamond-shaped pieces, some adorned with appliqué, some with patchwork. However, the one decorative aspect which all the patches have in common is the beautiful quilting. We have provided a trace pattern for one of the appliqué bird and flower motifs shown here, and you could use this for each urn. Alternatively, if you are confident at making up your own appliqué shapes, you could vary this design for each urn, adding butterflies or different shaped flowers and leaves.

1 Cutting out the templates Square up all patchwork templates (**a** to **m**) from Chart 1 on page 50 on to cardboard and cut out. Using templates (**a** and **j**), cut out 12 of each in magazine paper. Then also cut 24 each of templates (**b, d, e, f, g** and **h**), 48 each of template (**c**), 22 each of template (**k**), 4 each of template (**l**), finally, 6 each of template (**m**).

2 Cutting out the patches For each urn, pin one template (**a**) and two templates (**b, c, d,** and **h**) on to the wrong side of the same printed fabric, ensuring each template has a 6mm (¼in) seam allowance all round. Check that the fabric grain is straight on each piece and then cut out. Repeat to cut out all the pieces for the 12 urns, each in a different printed fabric. Next, cut out all the remaining templates in main fabric, with seam allowances added. Leave the templates (excluding **k, l** and **m**) pinned to the fabric patches for the next step.

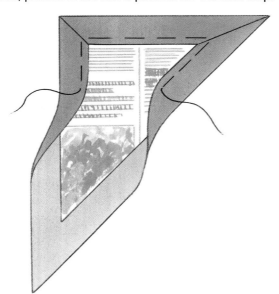

3 Tacking the patches Taking each of the cut-out shapes, fold the fabric seam allowances over the edges of the paper and pin, then tack all round the edges. Ensure the corners are neatly mitred, in order to create perfect angles.

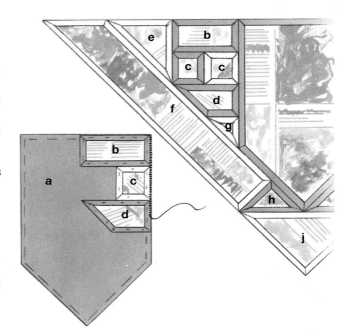

4 Making urn triangles The urn design is made up from patches (**a, b, c, d** and **h**) which are cut from the same printed fabric for each urn, while the background is made up of patches (**c, e, f, g** and **j**), which are all cut from main fabric. To make the urns, stitch patches together using Chart 1 as a guide. Begin by placing two patches together, right sides facing, and oversew neatly along the edge. Continue joining the patches together to make up 12 urn triangles.

5 Making up squares Place a triangle (**k**) over each urn triangle, with right sides facing and raw edges matching. Oversew pairs of triangles together along the longest edge, to form a square. Repeat to make up 12 squares, then remove all tacking and templates.

6 Adding the wadding Using template (**m**) as a pattern, cut out 18 in wadding. Then, using template (**k**), cut 10 in wadding, and cut four from template (**l**). Next, pair wadding pieces to wrong sides of the fabric pieces. Pin and tack all round and up and down each piece to secure wadding and fabric together.

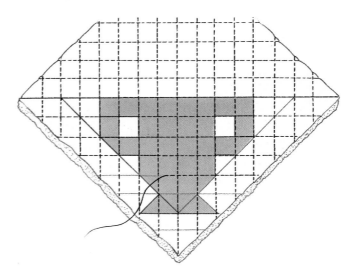

7 Quilting the trellis Taking each urn patchwork square, use tailor's chalk to draw up a trellis stitch guide, with parallel lines spaced 5cm (2in) apart. Then, machine quilt the trellis design all over the piece. Repeat for the other urn squares.

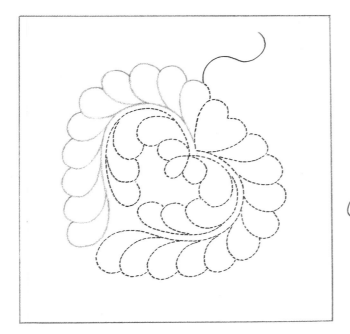

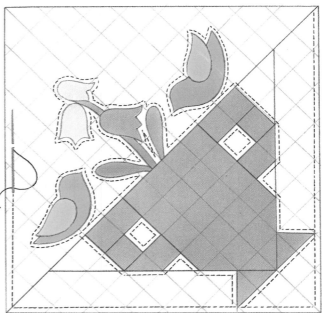

8 **Quilting the motifs** Square up pattern (**n**) and transfer to each plain wadded square (**m**) using blue tailor's chalk. Machine quilt the design following chalk lines, then repeat to machine stitch pattern (**o**) on to four wadded triangles (**k**), and (**p**) on to six wadded triangles (**k**). Finally, transfer pattern (**q**) on to the corner patches (**l**), and quilt as before. Stitch a basic trellis design over all the main fabric shapes, taking care not to stitch across the previously quilted motifs.

9 **Appliqué flowers and birds** Use patterns (**r** and **s**) and cut out in suitable colourways from the printed fabrics, with a 1cm (⅜in) seam allowance all round. You will require 12 flowers and 24 birds. Experiment with the colours until you are happy with the effect and then pin each fabric piece into position, using Chart 1 as a guide. Now, taking a needle with an appropriately coloured thread, fold the raw edges of the motif under to neaten and slipstitch all round the shape. Repeat in this way, until all the motifs are appliquéd into place.

10 **Quilting the urn squares** Place an urn square into a hoop and, taking a quilting needle with white thread, sew tiny running stitches through the wadding, around the outline of the urn, flowers and birds, finishing off with the border of the square. Ensure that the quilting stitches are straight and even for a neat finish. Repeat for the remaining urn squares.

Family emblem
Turn your quilt in to a real family heirloom, by quilting your family's crest on all, or alternate large squares, replacing the design. You could start by drawing entwined initials, then add this and a message in Latin to the centre of the heart-shaped design, to create your own family emblem.

MAKING UP THE QUILT

1 **Joining the squares** To make up, two diagonal strips each of 1, 3 and 5 squares are required. To join, place the squares with right sides facing, alternating the urn squares with the plain quilted squares and pin, then machine stitch together, taking a 6mm (¼in) seam allowance. Ensure that you always begin and end with an appliquéd urn patch.

2 **Joining the strips** Position the strips side by side, in the order in which they will be stitched to form the quilt. Position the quilted triangles (**k**) around the edges of the quilt, placing design (**p**) along the sides and design (**o**) along the upper and lower edges. Stitch a triangle to the end of each strip, then join the strips together. Finally, join triangles (**l**) to the four corners to create a perfect rectangle.

3 **Making up the border** Cut strips of the patterned fabric into 7.5cm (3in) widths, in varying lengths. Join together by pinning right sides together and then machine stitch to make two strips 120cm (48in) long and two more strips 170cm (58in) long. Now, with right sides facing, pin and machine stitch the short patchwork borders to the short ends of the quilt, taking a 6mm (¼in) seam allowance. Repeat to add the longer borders to the remaining edges of the quilt.

4 **Lining the quilt** Measure the outer edge of the quilt border and cut out the lining fabric to match these measurements. Place the quilt and lining fabric with right sides facing and pin and tack the border and lining together all round. Then machine stitch, taking a 6mm (¼in) seam allowance and leaving an opening in the lower edge to turn through to right sides. Snip off the corners of the seam allowances, turn to right sides and then slipstitch the opening closed.

Chart 1

Sleeping bag

Bedtime tears will be a thing of the past, and your children will be racing off to bed, if you give them the opportunity to sleep in this novelty sleeping bag. This wonderful man-in-the-moon bag would welcome anyone into the land of Nod, and perhaps, dreams of a journey on a starship. The features are first appliqued on to the cover, then the bag is stitched together. If you are feeling imaginative, you could even adapt the pattern and create a different fun character.

Choose washable fabrics and wadding of a suitable thickness. The bag is made from brushed cotton for a soft and cosy finish which feels lovely next to the skin. The man-in-the-moon cover is easy to make and if you choose ready quilted fabric it could be made up in no time at all. The finished size of the bag is around 120 x 72cm (48 x 28in).

▲ Stars in their eyes
Softly padded and very comfortable, this fun sleeping bag is very handy for little friends who visit and there's room for teddy too. The sleeping bag is made in a softly brushed cotton. To retain the mystery surrounding the man in the moon, keep the features in the same colour, but use darker shades to get the required definition.

MOON SLEEPING BAG

Materials

Main fabric brushed cotton, 5m x 140cm (198 x 55in)

Backing fabric 5m x 140cm (198 x 55in)

Wadding 5m x 140cm (198 x 55in) mediumweight

Fabric remnants two tones, for features

Bondaweb 20 x 120cm (8 x 47in) for attaching the features

Bias binding 4.5m x 2cm (178 x ¾in) to match the main fabric

Pattern paper, pencil and **tailor's chalk**

1 Cutting out Enlarge and draw the pattern pieces from the chart working to 1 square equals 10cm (4in). Add a 1.5cm (⅝ in) allowance and cut two of (**a**) body and (**b**) lower body in main, backing and wadding.

2 Quilting the fabric Place wadding on the wrong side of each corresponding fabric piece (**a** and **b**). Pin and tack the backing fabric to the wadding. Using tailor's chalk and a ruler, draw diagonal lines, 7cm (2¾in) apart, on to the right side of the main fabric pieces. Using the lines as a guide, quilt the fabric to form a basic trellis design.

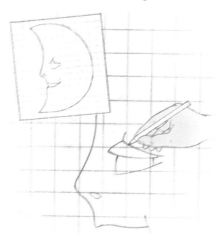

3 Tracing the features Enlarge and trace all the facial features from the chart on to Bondaweb. Then iron on to the appropriate coloured fabric and cut the eye lid, mouth and nostril pieces from the darkest colour remnant and cut the eyeball from the lighter colour remnant. Next iron all the features into place. Finally, satin stitch all round each feature.

4 Making up the cover With right sides facing and raw edges matching, place pieces (**b**) together and seam across the top edge, taking a 1.5cm (⅝in) allowance. Turn to right sides and topstitch along the seam, 1cm (⅜in) from the edge.

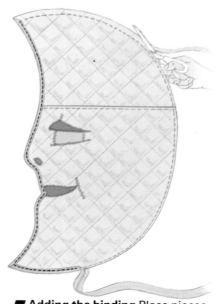

5 Adding the binding Place pieces (**a**), wrong sides together on to a flat surface, then lay the cover (**b**) on top. Pin and machine stitch together all round, taking a 1cm (⅜in) seam allowance. Trim seams, snip into the allowance and pin and tack the bias binding all round the edge. Taking care to ease the binding around the sharp corners, topstitch in place, keeping your stitching straight and enclosing raw edges.

▲ When the sandman comes
Young children will have hours of fun playing with this wonderful sleeping bag. And while they are asleep at night they can feel happy and safe knowing that the man in the moon is keeping watch over them through the dark night.

▼ *Chart for making the man-in-the-moon. Work to 1 square = 10cm (4in)*

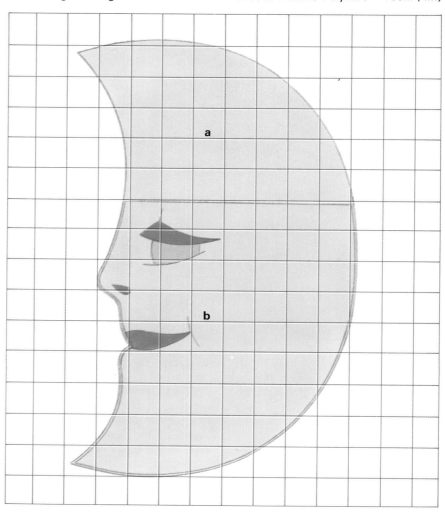

Quilted bedspreads

Quilting gives a bedspread body and shape, as well as providing extra warmth on chilly nights. Even the most basic quilted design, like the simple diamond pattern shown here, will show off your chosen fabric to the full.

When planning a quilt, take the colour and pattern of the fabric into account and choose a quilting pattern and sewing thread accordingly. If the fabric is covered with evenly spaced motifs, emphasize them by centring each one in its own quilted square or diamond. Stripes and checks can be quilted along or in-between their lines, or even at an angle to the main pattern. Plain glazed cottons look stunning quilted with thread in a darker shade, particularly if an intricate design is used, but for all-over patterns keep to a simple quilting design in a toning thread to avoid making the quilt too busy.

▲ **Quilted comfort**
The simplicity of the diamond quilting design on this bedspread is perfectly suited to the main fabric, giving it fullness and a luxuriously padded look, without detracting from the delicate floral pattern as a more elaborate design would.

Fabrics

Although ready-quilted fabric is available, the choice of fabric and the style of the quilting is limited. Quilting the fabric yourself gives you a far broader choice, allowing you not only to match the bedspread perfectly to other fabrics and colours in the bedroom, but also to experiment with the size and style of the quilted design to achieve different effects.

Firm, closely woven furnishing cottons are best for quilting large items such as bedspreads, as they provide the firm base needed for the stitching. Avoid sheer and loosely woven fabrics, which tend to become distorted when stitched, and through which the wadding underneath is often visible. The choice of fabric colour and pattern is virtually limitless, but do make sure that your chosen fabric is easy to launder, fairly crease-resistant and also reasonably hardwearing.

Joining fabric widths

If making a double, a king-size or even a floor-length single throw-over bedspread, it is unlikely that you will be able to buy fabric wide enough to make these from a single piece; to gain the required width you will need to seam together two or more widths of fabric. Rather than joining these with an unsightly central seam, use a full width of fabric for the centre of the bedspread, with two narrower widths (generally one full width of fabric cut in half lengthways) stitched to each side. Full details on joining fabric widths, and matching the pattern across the seam, are given in *Making a throw-over quilted bedspread* below.

Materials

Firm furnishing fabric the chosen size of the bedspread, plus a 1.5cm (⅝in) seam allowance all round (see the section on joining fabric widths)

Lining fabric the same size as the main fabric

Lightweight wadding the chosen size of the bedspread (see step 7 of *Making a throwover quilted bedspread*)

Covered piping cord (optional) to fit around the edges of the bedspread, plus 10-15cm (4-6in) for ease (see step 1 of *Trimming with piping* on page 56)

Sewing thread for quilting

Calculator, squared paper and **pencil** to draw up a small-scale plan of the quilt

Tailor's chalk, long ruler and **set square** to mark the quilting pattern on to the fabric

Tape measure

MAKING A THROWOVER QUILTED BEDSPREAD

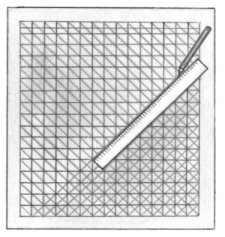

1 Measuring up Always measure up on a made-up bed as the cover will lie over all the bedlinen. First decide how far over the bed edges you want the cover to fall – midway down the side of the bed to reveal a pretty valance, or right to the floor to obscure stored objects or an ugly bed base and legs.

For the width, measure from the chosen depth on one side of the bed over to the same point on the opposite side of the bed. For the length, measure from just behind the pillow at the top of the bed down to the bottom end, taking the tape measure over the edge of the bed to the chosen depth.

Since quilting tends to reduce the overall size of the fabric add 10cm (4in) to both length and width measurements to compensate for this. Also, if you like to tuck the bed cover under the pillows to give a neat appearance, add a further 30cm (12in) to the length measurement.

2 Planning the pattern Decide roughly what size you would like the squares on your quilt to be – as a rough guide, they should be 12-20cm (4¾-8in). To calculate the exact square size needed to fit evenly into your bedspread, divide the width measurement by your desired square size to give the number of squares that will fit the measurement; round up the answer; then divide the measurement by the rounded-up number to give the exact square size.

For example: a bedspread width of 190cm (75in), divided by a square size of 15cm (6in), gives you 12.6 squares, or 13 whole squares when rounded up; divide 190cm (75in) by 13 to give you the exact square size of 14.6cm (5¾in).

As the bedspread is rectangular, you will almost always be left with incomplete squares on the length of the bedspread (if quilting on the diagonal, half-diamonds at the edges are inevitable); plan your bedspread so that incomplete squares lie along the top edge, where they can be hidden behind the pillows. Draw up a plan of the quilt on squared paper.

3 Cutting out If your fabric is wide enough to make the bedspread from a single piece, simply cut out a rectangle to the required size, adding a 1.5cm (⅝in) seam allowance all round. If you need to join two widths of fabric, cut one piece from the main fabric to the required length, plus a 3cm (1¼in) seam allowance at both ends, and a slightly longer piece to allow for pattern matching.

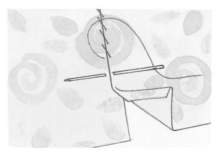

4 Joining widths Cut the longer length of fabric in half lengthways. Take one half-width and fold under 1.5cm (⅝in) to the wrong side along the selvedge; with right sides face up, position the folded edge of the half-width over one selvedge of the main fabric piece, overlapping the two by at least 1.5cm (⅝in) and matching the pattern if necessary. Slip-tack together: bring the needle up through the three layers of fabric on one side of the join, and out at the fold; make tiny stitches across the join through the single layer of fabric and the fold. Trim side pieces to same length as the main piece.

5 Stitching widths together Turn the side piece over to lie wrong side up, unfold the seam allowance and stitch through the centre of stitches formed along the folded edge. Remove tacking stitches. Attach second half-width to other side of panel. Snip into selvedges and press open. Trim equal amounts from sides to make quilt required width, plus a 1.5cm (⅝in) seam allowance on each side.

6 Marking the pattern Lay the top fabric out flat, with right side up. Use tailor's chalk and a long ruler to mark out the quilting design on the fabric, using your mini-plan as a guide. Begin by marking out the longest diagonals, then mark up all the shorter diagonals, making sure they are perfectly parallel and at an equal distance apart. Use a set square to ensure that all the angles of the diamonds are perfect right angles. If you can use a quilting bar confidently, do not chalk in every line, but only the main diagonals and a few others as reference points.

7 Joining widths of wadding To make up a piece of wadding the same size as the bedspread, you will probably need to join widths together. Line up the wadding pieces, with side edges butting, and stitch together with a wide herringbone stitch.

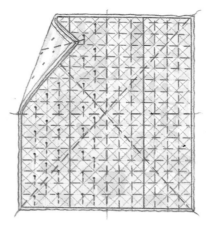

8 Seaming the wadding Lay the wadding out flat and centre the main fabric over it, right side up. Starting at the centre of the bedspread, pin and tack out to the corners and to the middle of each side edge. Then pin and tack a series of parallel lines 20cm (8in) apart, running across the quilt from one side to the other, and down it from top to bottom; you will find that the wadding spreads out a little as you tack. Finally, pin and tack around the outer edges of the quilt.

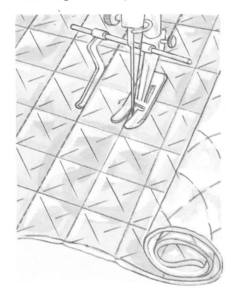

9 Quilting the fabric Experiment on spare pieces of fabric and wadding to find a suitable stitch size – you will need to use a size slightly larger than average. With the fabric face up, begin the quilting by straight-stitching along one of the two longest diagonals, following the chalked line (see machine-quilting tips). Then swing the quilt round and straight-stitch along the other longest diagonal.

Following the chalked pattern and, if you have one, using a quilting bar set to the desired distance, stitch along all the diagonals going in one direction, before swinging the quilt round and stitching along those running in the opposite direction.

If you are quilting a particularly large bedspread, work the longer diagonals from the centre of the quilt out to the edges. Remove all the tacking stitches.

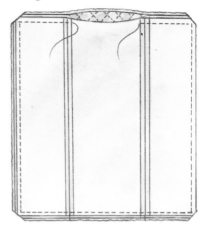

10 Attaching the lining Make up the lining to the same size as the bedspread, including a 1.5cm (⅝in) seam allowance all round, joining widths if necessary.

Lay out the quilted fabric, fabric side face up, and place the lining over it, matching the edges and with right sides together. Pin, tack and stitch round the edges, taking a 1.5cm (⅝in) seam allowance and leaving a 45cm (18in) opening in the middle of one edge.

Trim the corners and seams, cutting off the wadding close to the stitching, and turn the bedspread through to the right side. Turn in the opening edges and slip-stitch them together.

tip

Machine-quilting
Supporting the fabric When machine-quilting a large item like a bedspread, make sure the bulk of the quilt is supported as you stitch. If it is allowed to hang free over the edge of the table, it will pull during stitching and result in uneven stitch lengths; either work on a very large table or drape the bedspread over a second table or chair.
Working the centre To work the centre of the bedspread, keep the sides rolled up, with the largest section of quilt to the left of the machine foot, and the smaller section tightly rolled to fit under the arm of the sewing machine. If the bedspread is very large, work it from the centre out to the edges, rather than from one side to the other.

TRIMMING WITH PIPING

Trimming the bedspread with fabric-covered piping gives you the opportunity to link it to other fabrics and colours in the bedroom, as well as giving the outline of the quilt added definition and a professional finish.

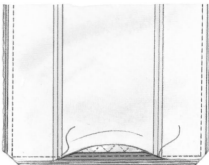

1 Making the piping Make up the quilt as usual, following steps 1-9. Measure right the way round the outer edge of the quilt to assess how much piping is needed. Make up fabric-covered piping to the required length, plus 10-15cm (4-6in) for ease; use fairly thick piping cord, with a toning or contrast fabric for the bias strips.

2 Attaching the piping Lay out the quilt, with fabric side face up. Pin and tack the covered piping around the edges of the bedspread, with the cord lying innermost and with the stitching line along the piping 1.5cm (⅝in) from the outer edge of the bedspread; to help the piping fabric lie flat, snip into it at the corners, up to the stitching line.

3 Finishing the quilt Make up the lining as usual and place it over the bedspread, matching the edges and with right sides together. Pin, tack and stitch round the bedspread edges through all layers, taking a 1.5cm (⅝in) seam allowance, and leaving a 45cm (18in) opening in the middle of one edge. At the opening, stitch through all layers except the lining. Remove tacking stitches, trim corners and seams, and turn the bedspread through to the right side. Turn in the open edges and slip-stitch the lining to the main fabric.

▼ *Topping idea*
Added length allows this quilted cover to tuck beneath the pillows.

Pattern quilting

Quilting has always been valued as much for its decorative appeal as for its more practical qualities of warmth and durability. It gives a fabric body and volume, and can also enhance the design if used to outline single motifs or the overall pattern. Emphasize the images on a floral fabric by quilting around flowers and leaves, or stitch around the shapes and splashes of colour in an abstract design to add impact.

Although quilting around motifs is less straightforward than quilting a basic trellis design, it can still easily be done by machine, provided the motifs are not too small and intricate. If your fabric is patterned with large and small motifs, only quilt the former to make up the dominant part of the design. If you wish, the more delicate motifs can be quilted afterwards, either by hand or machine.

With a strong or elaborate pattern, use a thread that blends in with the background; on more subtle designs, accent the motif outlines with a contrasting colour. For items like a bedspread, use a firm, closely woven furnishing cotton, which gives a firm base for the quilting. Make sure that your chosen fabric is easy to clean and reasonably hardwearing.

▼ Freestyle quilting
Stitching around the motifs on a fabric brings its design to life, giving it body and movement. Follow the outlines of each motif, or deviate from them slightly to create complementary patterns.

▲ Textured flowers *The leaf and floral motifs on these bedspreads have been carefully quilted, giving the fabric design a textured, three-dimensional effect.*

Materials

Firm furnishing cotton – see steps 1 and 2 for quantity
Lining fabric the same size as the main fabric
Backing fabric for quilting, the same size as the main fabric
Lightweight 2oz wadding the same size as the main fabric
Sewing thread for quilting
Tape measure
Scissors

QUILTED MOTIF BEDSPREAD

1 Measuring up Make sure the bed is fully made up before you begin to measure it. Decide how far over the edge of the bed you would like the cover to fall – midway down the base or right to the floor. For the length, measure from just behind the pillows down to the bottom of the bed, taking the tape measure over to the required depth. For the width, measure from the required depth on one side of the bed over to the same point on the opposite side.

2 Cutting out When you have established the finished size of bedspread, cut out the fabric to the correct size, adding a further 6cm (2½in) all round for seams and shrinkage during quilting; join fabric widths where necessary, making sure you match the pattern across the seams. If you wish to tuck the bedspread under the front of the pillows for a neater appearance, add a further 30cm (12in) to the length. Cut out and make up the lining fabric and the wadding to the same size. (For full details on joining fabric and wadding widths, see pages 54–55.)

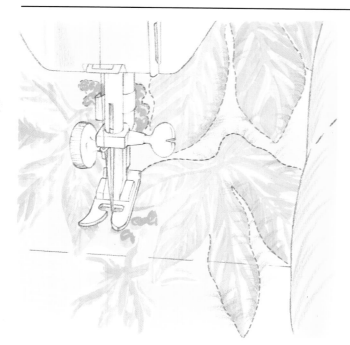

5 Stitching around the motif Carefully stitch around the outline of your chosen motif, trying to maintain a steady rhythm and speed – this will be easier if you plan your stitching sequence in advance. When stitching around sharp curves and points, such as leaf tips, make sure you stitch right to the edge of the motif, and pivot the needle to avoid distorting the fabric.

6 Emphasizing the design To add further interest and emphasis to the motifs, quilt in any details that immediately catch your eye, such as the edges of the petals within a rose motif, or the veins on a leaf. As well as adding a touch of realism, this will give the bedspread a wonderfully textured appearance. For natural motifs, like flowers, use a matching thread to fill in detail, so that the eye is drawn to the enhanced design rather than the colour of the thread.

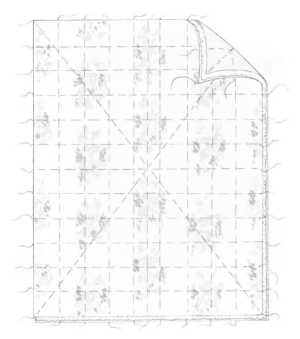

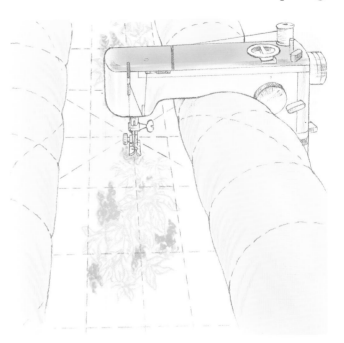

3 Tacking the wadding to the fabric Sandwich the wadding between the backing fabric and the main fabric, with the main fabric right side up. Starting at the centre of the bedspread, pin and tack through all layers, working out to each corner, and then to the middle of each side edge. Then pin and tack a series of lines across and down the quilt, spaced about 20cm (8in) apart, to form a grid.

4 Getting started Before you begin, practise quilting around motifs on a spare piece of fabric and wadding, until you find the correct stitch length and tension. When you are satisfied, it's best to start with a fairly large motif at the centre of the bedspread. Tightly roll up the sides of the quilt and slip one roll under the arm of the sewing machine – this will make it easier for you to manipulate the quilt while working the centre. If possible work on a large table.

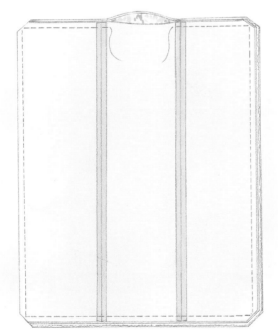

7 Attaching the lining Quilt the whole bedspread, working from the centre out to the edges. Then lay out the quilted bedspread with the right side up, and centre the lining over it, with right sides together. Pin and stitch round the edges, taking a 1.5cm (⅝in) seam allowance and leaving a 45cm (18in) opening in the middle of one edge. Trim the corners and seam allowances, then turn through to the right side. Turn in the opening edges and slipstitch together. (For details on piping the bedspread, see page 56.)

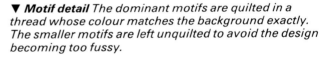

▼ **Motif detail** *The dominant motifs are quilted in a thread whose colour matches the background exactly. The smaller motifs are left unquilted to avoid the design becoming too fussy.*

Quilted appliqué

By combining your quilting skills with basic appliqué, you can create stylish fabric borders for a set of pillowcases. For fully co-ordinated bedlinen, use motifs from leftover bedspread fabric, or from a similar design. Quilting the motifs before you appliqué them to the pillowcases gives them a soft, contoured look, perfectly suited to plump pillows.

Make up a design from a series of motifs scattered down the side of the pillow or, for a more subtle effect, use a single motif in a corner. On a small project like a pillowcase, hand-quilting is always an option, so feel free to choose dainty, intricate motifs. For comfort's sake, always stitch motifs down the side of the pillowcase.

MOTIF PILLOWCASES

1 Cutting out the motifs Plan a rough design and decide which motifs you want to use. Roughly cut out each motif from the main fabric, leaving a 5cm (2in) border all round. For each motif, cut out a piece of wadding and one of backing fabric to the same size.

2 Stitching the motifs Sandwich the wadding between the backing fabric and the wrong side of the motif, and pin and tack together around edges. Straight stitch round the motif, carefully following its outline and stitching through all layers. Stitch in any detail within the motif as well, to add interest and texture. Trim the fabric and wadding to just outside the stitching line.

3 Attaching the motifs Pin each motif separately in position on the pillowcase, arranging the design to achieve the best effect. If the pillowcases are intended to match the bedspread, place the motifs in a similar layout as the original pattern. Use a machine or handworked satin stitch to stitch the motifs in place, working round the outside of each one and covering the raw fabric edges.

 tip

Relief effect
To create different areas of relief on a motif, add layers of wadding or cut sections away; for example, give the petals of flowers a fuller effect by cutting wadding away at their base.

▼▶ Sweet dreams
Plain pillowcases are greatly enhanced by the addition of quilted motifs. If short of time, simply stitch a strip of decorative fabric, down the side of the pillowcase to create an equally stylish effect.